Ivan the Terrible

A Captivating Guide to the First Tsar of Russia and His Impact on Russian History

Free Bonus from Captivating History (Available for a Limited time)

Hi History Lovers!

Now you have a chance to join our exclusive history list so you can get your first history ebook for free as well as discounts and a potential to get more history books for free! Simply visit the link below to join.

Captivatinghistory.com/ebook

Also, make sure to follow us on Facebook, Twitter and Youtube by searching for Captivating History.

Contents

Introduction

Considering that he has gone down in history as Ivan the Terrible, the first tsar of Russia could hardly have been a Boy Scout. As his name suggests, Ivan had an utterly terrifying presence during his thirty-seven-year-long reign.

Starting with his first execution at the tender age of thirteen when he had a nobleman thrown into a cage full of starving dogs and watched as the man was ripped to pieces, Ivan has had a reputation for brutality that is founded in horrifying truth. He massacred an entire city, poisoned his own wife, tortured small animals, and killed thousands of innocent people in frighteningly cruel and unusual ways. Peasants or nobles, family or strangers—Ivan cared little as long as he could kill. He married eight wives, raped hundreds of other women, and abdicated his responsibilities not once but twice. The first time he returned only when he was granted absolute power, and he abused it viciously by forming the terrifying *Oprichniki*, a regiment of ruthless horsemen who murdered anyone that stood in Ivan's way. The second time, he placed an enemy general on the throne and worshiped him for a year before ousting him and taking back his position as tsar.

Ivan's wild actions have led scholars and historians to label him as a psychopath and a deeply disturbed individual. There is no disputing the fact that Ivan's mental health was questionable at best. It would be all too easy to call him a monster, all too simple to believe that a human being could not have conceivably committed the heinous crimes that Ivan took such pleasure in. But once one starts to delve deeper into the psyche of one of the worst monarchs in all of history, there is more to see than just a cold-blooded killer.

Ivan's story is not only one of brutality, but it is also a tale of great suffering. It's the story of a little boy whose father died when he was just a toddler; a story of a child whose mother was poisoned when he was only seven years old. This was a boy who had to struggle to survive as the warring nobility threatened, molested, and harassed him endlessly while he tried to protect his only friend—his deaf and mute little brother. This is also the tale of a young man who was desperate for power to defend himself and found it when he was made the tsar. And it's almost the story of a good and capable ruler whose wild temper was soothed by the presence of a tsaritsa who seemed capable of calming the storm that was Ivan's mind; but, sadly, Ivan's beloved first wife was poisoned and died in agony, plunging him into a cauldron of darkness and depression that produced the tyrant that has gone down in history as a monster.

He was not a monster, however. He was a man. And this is his story.

Chapter 1 – Russia Before the First Tsar

The Slavs, Finns, and some other tribes were in trouble, and they knew it.

Even though they had driven the Varangians out of their small towns and villages when they first arrived and briefly occupied their villages some years ago, some of the people were murmuring that things had been better when the tall Scandinavians had been in charge of their territories. They had arrived peacefully in their mighty longboats, these great, bearded men with powerful arms and warlike figures, which had been enough to scare the tribes. While the Varangians were peaceful, the Slavs and others knew that this was just because they didn't have anything to steal. Their lands, however, did. They were abundant and fertile, filled with treasures that the Varangian merchants could take and sell all over the world: beeswax and furs, honey and timber. Fearing exploitation, the Slavic people drove the Varangians out, and now they began to settle down to govern themselves.

Yet this proved to be more difficult than they'd expected. The unity that had bound them together in order to defeat their new enemies disappeared the moment the last Varangian longboat sailed back to the distant lands from where it came. As soon as they no longer had a common foe to fight against, they fell to fighting one another. By the late 9th century CE, the country of Russia was in chaos. Trade fell apart as the tribes couldn't agree on anything until a single solution came to the people: Get the Varangians back to unify them, this time in peace instead of in war.

When the Slavs and Finns from the land surrounding the Lovat and Volkhov Rivers realized this, they decided to take action. They sent a message to Scandinavia asking the Varangians to come back and govern them. At least, this is what happened according to the *Russian Primary Chronicle*, a selection of texts possibly compiled by the Russian monk Nestor the Chronicler in the early 11th century. Other sources suggest that the Varangians likely arrived and attacked Russia by force, citing Nestor's pro-Norman slant as reason to doubt his compilation. Either way, in 862, three Varangian brothers arrived in the area that now contains parts of modern-day Belarus, Russia, and Ukraine.

The eldest of the three brothers was Rurik. While many of the Slavic and Finno-Ugric peoples accepted him immediately as their ruler, others resisted, and Rurik took up his two-edged Viking blade and forged himself a kingdom in this new territory. With the backup of his Varangian soldiers as well as his native allies, he forced his opponents back. Even the deaths of both of Rurik's brothers didn't stop him; he simply absorbed their territories into his own.

Rurik established the seat of his government by building a settlement that he named Novgorod, which translates to "new fortification." Despite the fact that there were larger cities in the region at the time, it was in Novgorod that he would return to live out his later years. Here he finally settled, content with the kingdom that he had made for himself.

Little did Rurik know that one of his descendants would, hundreds of years later, sow utter terror through the very streets of the new city that he had just finished building.

* * * *

Rurik was the founder of the first great dynasty of unified Russian rulers. Before his arrival, Russia had been occupied for hundreds of years primarily by wandering nomadic tribes that lived off its vast and fertile lands without establishing any central government. These tribes included the people that were known to the rest of the world as the Scythians. They occupied the great steppes in the south and were a warlike people and renowned horsemen—in fact, the Scythians likely came up with the idea of castrating male horses, a practice that would revolutionize the use of horses both in war and in peace, as the resultant geldings were far more tractable than stallions without losing their strength and size.

It was ancient Greek merchants who would first stumble upon these tribes and connect them to the rest of the world via trade. Ancient Rome also had its stake in Russian dealings when Nero made some Russian lands part of his Moesia Inferior province, but most attempts to conquer Russia ended in disaster as wild nomadic tribes, such as the Huns, would invariably arrive. It was only in the 6th century that the Khazars would arrive and tame some of those wild steppes. The Khazars were a fairly peaceful people; they became Jews somewhere between 700 and 800 and drew much of their power from their alliance with the Byzantine Empire.

Rurik's arrival, however, ushered in a new era: that of the Kievan Rus'. After his death in 879, one of his relatives, Oleg, rose to power. Oleg's goal was to expand the territories that his late kinsman had amassed. He first set his sights on Smolensk, a city that functioned as a center of trade between two major rivers, the Dnieper and the Western Dvina. After successfully conquering it, Oleg headed for the bigger target of Kiev, located along the Dnieper itself. The city had long been oppressed by the Khazars, who demanded high tribute from the Kievans; however, two men from Rurik's original band, Askold and Dir, had since overtaken the city and started their own reigns of terror over it. The men, true to their Viking origins, started to launch raids on the surrounding regions, using Kiev as their base. Nestor speculates that they might even have attacked

Constantinople, the capital of the Byzantine Empire; either way, they wrought havoc on Kiev and its surroundings.

Oleg tricked Askold and Dir into emerging from the city and killed them both. Kiev was fairly welcoming toward Oleg and even more so when he persuaded them to stop paying tribute to the Khazars. Surrounding cities followed suit, and by the time of Oleg's death, he had expanded his lands to a large political federation known as the Kievan Rus'.

* * * *

Once Oleg had firmly established the Kievan Rus', the federation was cast into an era of turbulence and turmoil. Igor, the son of Rurik, became its next leader; he was greedy for wealth and taxed his people too harshly, ending up being assassinated by the Drevlian tribe. His wife, Olga, used trickery and violence to kill many Drevlians in revenge during her subsequent regency, going to incredible lengths in her grief and rage. She eventually abdicated in 963, plunging the Rus' into chaos. While her son, Sviatoslav I, succeeded in expanding the territory somewhat, he was assassinated on his way home to Kiev after a battle, and his three sons squabbled over the territory.

One of the sons, Vladimir, was forced to hide out in Norway as his two brothers threatened to destroy the Rus' and each other in their quest for power. While they fought, Vladimir amassed an army of followers. His marriage to Anne, the sister of Byzantine Emperor Basil II, provided him with a powerful ally. He returned, conquered his brothers, and took control of the Rus'.

Vladimir's rule proved to be a golden age for the Kievan Rus'. The predominantly pagan nation was converted to Eastern Orthodox Christianity, which brought more unity to the people, and Vladimir promoted education and the arts. Schools, cities, and churches were built, trade with the Byzantine Empire boomed, and when Vladimir died in 1015, he was known as Vladimir the Great.

His oldest son, Sviatopolk, briefly ruled the Rus' for four chaotic years, murdering three of his brothers to cling onto his power. Another brother, Yaroslav, succeeded in deposing the bloodthirsty ruler, and he brought about another era of peace and expansion. Improving on his laws, borders, and relations with surrounding countries as important as Sweden and the Byzantine Empire, Yaroslav earned his title of Yaroslav the Wise.

Unfortunately, Yaroslav was the last great leader of the Kievan Rus'. His greatest mistake was made on his deathbed when he divided his territory among his sons, perhaps trying to avoid the grief and terror that fighting among his own brothers had caused him and his people. The move had the opposite effect to what he'd intended. Fragmented, the Rus' fell into a squabbling mess and eventually fell apart.

Its borders fractured, Russia was rendered instantly vulnerable to outside attack. It was overrun by the marauding Mongols in 1223, and while they established important infrastructure such as roads, their oppressive influence would last for decades. It was only in the late 13th century that a new dynasty would rise to power, and it would be brought about by a hero from the very city that Rurik had first chosen for his seat of power: Novgorod.

Chapter 2 – A Lineage of Heroes

Illustration I: Aleksandr Nevsky at the Battle of the Neva, a painting by Boris Artemievich Tchorikov

The frozen surface of the lake was still and smooth, coated in snow, but Aleksandr Nevsky knew that its appearance was deceptive. In reality, the ice's surface was uneven and treacherous—and he was counting on it.

He could hear the heavy breathing of his men and horses all around him. Already, ice jangled in the coats of the horses as they moved, their sweat frozen into their long, shaggy winter coats. Aleksandr knew that his own mustache was frosted as his breath steamed and hung in the air. He sucked in the smell of the sweating animals, of the crisp winter day, of the blood. They had fought hard already, and the hardest fighting was still to come.

Aleksandr's hope, however, lay in the lake before him. Once their Crusader enemies had put him and his army to flight—a purposeful retreat calculated to lure them to a battlefield of Aleksandr's choosing—he had taken his swift cavalry and light infantry and fled out of sight, then led them across the creaking, popping surface of the lake. Aleksandr knew that lake like the back of his hand, and he was able to get his men to safety, picking their way across the treacherous surface. The ice at the very edge of the shore was broken and scattered, but the water was only knee-deep. His enemies, however, had little idea that the lake was even there. They wouldn't know about it until they were upon it—and that was exactly what Aleksandr was counting on. His retreat had been nothing but a calculated move to lead his enemies to the battleground of his own choosing.

There was a great roar from the white horizon. Aleksandr's men snapped to attention; he could hear their breathing increase, feel the heartbeat of his own war pony speed up between his knees where he sat on its broad, hairy back. The next moment, the horizon bristled with lances, the banner of the Teutonic Knights snapping and curling against the gray winter sky. The banner bore a yellow cross and a rampant bird, its beak and claws blood red and ready for battle. But it failed to strike fear into the heart of Aleksandr Nevsky. He had beaten the Swedes at the Neva, outnumbered as he was, in 1240, and he knew his army was larger than that of the Teutonic Knights; he was more than ready to face them.

A great horn sounded, and hooves crunched and thundered on the ice. The knights were charging. Forming a wedge shape, the Crusader army bore down upon the Russians, their horses snorting and laboring through the deep snow in their heavy armor. Aleksandr's lines held, but he heard the creak of bowstrings as his horse archers got ready for the fight.

The leader of the Crusaders reached the lake. Aleksandr saw his horse slip and falter, its hooves unsure on the ice. The lines of approaching knights ebbed momentarily as their horses hesitated at the unfamiliar footing then surged forward once more. But the hammer of thousands of hooves on the frozen lake made it creak and moan, the gentler sounds of its agony underlining the bellowing horns of the approaching army.

From the Russian ranks came the order to fire. As one, the horse archers let loose with their small, compact bows. Arrows arced through the air, a rain of devastation that crashed upon the knights. The clang of arrowheads on armor was not the only noise that filled the air now. There was a great splintering crack, and Aleksandr saw a horse simply disappear, a spray of icy water swallowing it and its rider as they tumbled through the ice.

They were not the only ones. But most of the knights had made it, despite their slipping, stumbling horses, and the Russian infantry had to brace themselves. Another volley of arrows flew from the horse archers, and then the knights had reached them. There was a great crash, and the Battle on the Ice had begun.

* * * *

Aleksandr Yaroslavich, born in May 1220, was just a nineteen-year-old kid when he won the Battle of the Neva against all odds on July 15th, 1240. His victory stopped the large-scale Swedish invasion of Russia in its tracks and made him an instant hero, earning him the new surname of Nevsky, meaning "of Neva." He had been born into a chaotic chapter in the history of Russia, then called the Republic of Novgorod. The Mongols had invaded Russia and sown terrible destruction throughout the country, and the Crusaders came close on their heels, bent on converting the Eastern Orthodox Russians to the Catholic faith of the Western countries. Still staggering from the blows the Mongols had dealt them, the Russians were hardly prepared for the Crusaders to attack their borders.

However, Aleksandr Nevsky rose to the challenge. When the Crusader army met the Russians on the frozen surface of Lake Peipus in 1242, it's true that many of the knights fell through the ice, but Aleksandr's tactics were largely to thank for the Russian victory that took place there that day. The Crusaders were thrown back, and to this day, the lake remains part of the boundary between Russia and Estonia. Aleksandr's victory echoes through the centuries.

This would not be his only contribution to history. His military prowess made him a popular leader with the people, and despite being a man of war, he made efforts to make peace with the Mongols even though this left the Republic of Novgorod paying tribute to the Mongolian leader, Sartaq Khan. Aleksandr's good relations with Khan eventually earned him the title of Grand Prince of Vladimir— the ruler of all Russia. And so began a dynasty that would produce many great leaders, including one who would be called "the Terrible."

* * * *

Aleksandr's oldest son, Dmitri, became grand prince after his father's death in 1263. This left little power for Aleksandr's youngest, Daniil Aleksandrovich, to inherit, but he solved this problem by founding the Grand Duchy of Moscow, a new principality over which he would rule. Little did Daniil know that, over time, Moscow would grow to be bigger than its parent state of Vladimir, eventually becoming the most important duchy of Russia.

It was a Grand Prince of Moscow—Dmitri Donskoy, the great-great-grandson of Aleksandr Nevsky—who would eventually throw off the shackles of Mongol oppression, routing his enemies at the Don River in 1380. While Mongolia still required tribute from Russia, the

Mongols now knew that they had to treat Russia with respect, and their oppression did decline somewhat. Dmitri's actions solidified Moscow's position as the seat of Russian leadership.

Four generations later, Ivan the Great would finish what Dmitri had started. Born in 1440, he was known as Ivan III when he took his place as the Grand Prince of Moscow in 1462. Despite the fact that he was still a young man when he ascended to the throne, Ivan had been a co-ruler with his blind father since he was just a child, and he would soon display exactly how wise his years of experience had already made him.

His first achievement was to annex Novgorod, which had been a separate republic previously. This started off a chain of conquests and annexations with Russia's borders being pushed farther and farther back until, by the end of Ivan's reign, his country was three times the size that it had been when he took the throne. Still, this was not enough for the prince. Every new town that he captured was another chunk of tribute that he had to pay the Mongols, and knowing that their power was already slipping away from them, Ivan knew that the time was right to break free of them once and for all. In 1480—ten years after conquering Novgorod—Ivan refused to pay tribute. Displaying his prowess as a tactful diplomat as well as a strong warrior, Ivan succeeded in establishing Russia's independence peacefully. He maintained good relations with the leader of the Mongols and piloted Russia safely into a new era of independence.

The greatest disappointment of Ivan's reign was the ongoing war with Lithuania. Despite the fact that Ivan had easily conquered many of the other regions bordering Russia, Lithuania proved difficult, which was not helped when the heir to the Russian throne rebelled against him. Ivan had decided to nominate his grandson, Dmitri, as heir to the throne, but Ivan's own son and Dmitri's uncle, Vasili, was deeply unhappy with this decision and became a rebel. He defected to Lithuania and threatened to cause further chaos for his aging father, prompting Ivan to imprison the innocent Dmitri and bring Vasili back as the heir.

In 1505, Ivan III the Great died peacefully, and Vasili III became the Grand Prince of Moscow, despite the drama and chaos that had surrounded the succession. Little did either of them know that this would not be the last time that a Grand Prince of Moscow had trouble when it came to his family. As much as Ivan had been great, a second Ivan was about to ascend—and this one would be known not as the Great but as the Terrible.

Chapter 3 – The Birth of an Emperor

Illustration II: The Ascension Church in Kolomenskoye

Vasili III had been waiting for a son.

The son of Ivan the Great, Vasili had so far had a fairly peaceful reign as the Grand Prince of Moscow. Spending most of his time consolidating and firmly establishing the policies that his father had put into place, Vasili's uneventful rule would later earn him the mocking nickname of Vasili the Adequate. Yet one thing was missing, and it weighed heavily on his heart. Vasili was forty-seven, and he still had no son to whom he could leave the throne. He had been trying to limit the power of the nobility—the boyars—for most of his rule, but he was still horribly conscious that they were a selfish, squabbling bunch who mostly wanted to gain wealth and power for themselves. Despite Vasili's difficult behavior as a younger man, he was now trying to follow in his father's footsteps, and he knew that leaving the princedom to the chaotic boyars would be disastrous for the people.

The other option was for him to nominate one of his two surviving brothers as heirs to the throne, but Vasili didn't trust them—although to be fair, he didn't trust anyone; his multiple executions of those nobles who dared to criticize him serve as evidence for his paranoia.

No, there was only one option for an heir: Vasili had to produce a son. And here was where the grand prince found himself failing. His wife, Solomonia Saburova, was no longer a young woman. Despite twenty years of marriage—as well as countless pilgrimages and other attempts to banish the curse of infertility that seemed determined to cling to her barren womb—Solomonia had never been able to conceive a child. Breaking tradition and even canonical law, Vasili divorced Solomonia and sought a younger woman to become his wife, eventually settling on Elena Glinskaya. She was the young and beautiful daughter of a Serbian princess, and Vasili was head over heels in love with her, even though at 47 he would have hardly stood a chance with her if not for his title. She was stunning, and Vasili decided she would be the one to produce his heir.

Despite the general disapproval of the population, Vasili married Elena among great festivities in the winter of 1526. Now, at last, there would be a son and heir to the throne of Moscow—or at least, so Vasili and his new young wife hoped. But the years began to slip past, and with every month that slid away from him, Elena's womb remained stubbornly empty, and Vasili's heart sank more and more. Would he die childless after all, leaving Russia to his irresponsible brothers and the selfish boyars? The people began to murmur that

God had cursed Elena with infertility as punishment for Vasili's divorce of Solomonia.

At last, in the summer of 1530, Elena's belly began to swell and then to bulge. It seemed that Vasili was going to become a father after all, but whether or not he would have an heir remained to be seen; if this child was a girl, the throne would still be in a tenuous position.

Elena gave birth at last on August 25th, 1530. The thin cry of a newborn child rose into the air of the Kolomenskoye, the royal estate of the grand prince, and hope rang across all of Russia as Vasili prayed that his offspring would be a son. And it was: a little boy had come into the world, heir to the throne of Moscow.

Ivan was born to tremendous celebrations, the future of Russia secure due to his birth. To commemorate his birth, his father commanded a beautiful church to be built in gleaming white stone; this Ascension Church still stands in the Kolomenskoye today, the oldest surviving structure on the estate.

For the first few years of Ivan's life, relative peace and prosperity characterized his existence. Doted on by his mother, Ivan was given only the very best that Moscow could offer. Two years after Ivan's birth, Elena bore him a little brother named Yuri; now Ivan had a little playmate too, and the toddler's life would have been picturesque on the majestic grounds of the Kolomenskoye, playing under the shadow of the very church that was built to commemorate his birth.

Ivan was only three years old when his life took a sudden and brutal turn for the worse. His father, Vasili, had seldom been home throughout Ivan's short life. The war with Lithuania that had started during the reign of Ivan's grandfather was still raging, and while Vasili's army had been able to capture the important strategic town of Smolensk, he still spent much of his time at war.

It was not in battle, however, that Vasili would fall. Instead, it was a hobby that would bring about his demise. Hunting was a favorite pastime for much of the Russian nobility. They often used birds of prey—a practice known as "hawking," although most Russians hunted with falcons—or pursued their quarry on horseback with hunting dogs. The elegant, curly-coated borzoi is a modern example of the hunting hounds that the boyars bred hundreds of years ago. Bears, wolves, and foxes were some examples of the big game that was popular for hunting at the time, but Vasili's favorite quarry was the hare. Riding his swift hunting horse, he could follow the hounds for hours, watching the tiny brown form of the hare skimming across the snowy landscape ahead of him as hounds, men, and steeds stretched themselves to their limits to catch up.

Hunting was Vasili's escape from the wars, politics, and everything else that plagued the mind of a grand prince. But it was also on a hunting trip that he would hear his own death knell.

* * * *

It was a perfect winter's day in late November of 1533. Vasili was only fifty-four years old, and he had ridden out with his retinue to go for a hunting expedition near Volokolamsk, about eighty miles from Moscow. Vasili's horse's breath steamed in the cold air as the big animal trotted through the snow, its slender legs sinking deep into the drifts as Vasili strained his eyes looking for the hounds. Where were they? He could hear their baying; they couldn't be far from the hare now.

Vasili felt good about the turns his life had taken lately. While there was still not yet peace with Lithuania, at least he had two little boys and a pretty young wife waiting for him back in the Kolomenskoye, and now he was enjoying a perfect day's hunt, as carefree as the hounds that ran and barked across the snow. Despite the pressures of his position, Vasili was a little relaxed for once.

Then he felt it. A terrible, stabbing, blazing pain in his right hip, as if a hot poker had been forcibly shoved into his flesh. Gasping with pain, Vasili reined in his horse, trembling in agony. His retinue gathered anxiously around him, and the grand prince confessed that he could go no farther. He was in too much pain.

The nearest village of Kolp was only a short ride away, but by the time they reached the village, Vasili was doubled over his horse's mane, ashen with pain. He was hurried inside, and two German doctors were called to examine him. Tossing and thrashing, fevered and in agony on his bed, the grand prince fought for his life as the doctors rushed to his aid. They found an abscess on his hip, angry and swollen, the red welts traveling in all directions from the infected lump telling them that the infection had spread. Vasili had blood poisoning.

Even now, there is little that modern medicine can do for severe septic patients. Almost five hundred years ago, the doctors' hands were practically tied. They may have tried bloodletting, using a poultice of herbs on the abscess, given the grand prince alcohol in a bid to ease his pain, or they may have even attached fistfuls of leeches to Vasili's skin, hoping that the slimy creatures would suck the infection out of his blood. None of this worked though. Knowing that he was dying, Vasili asked to be taken back to Moscow and his family.

Vasili and his retinue made it back to Moscow on November 25th, 1533. By then, the grand prince would have been very sick, ridden with a fluctuating fever that gave him only brief respites before returning with a terrible vengeance. No amount of bloodletting could have ever helped him; in fact, if his physicians continued trying this treatment, he likely only grew sicker from the loss of blood. Yet nobody knew any better. Nobody could help him.

And so, in the middle of the night on December 4th, 1533, Vasili III Ivanovich perished in the city that he loved. Little Ivan was just a toddler, but already he was no longer heir to the title of Grand Prince: he *was* the Grand Prince of Moscow.

Chapter 4 – Assassination

Vasili was buried in the Cathedral of the Archangel in Moscow, a magnificent, soaring building topped with roofs that glistened like gold in the sun. Wide-eyed, the innocent little Ivan would not have understood the great pomp and ceremony surrounding the burial. All he knew was that his father was gone—although considering that Ivan probably barely knew his father, this may not have had a huge effect on his young life.

Elena was a more important figure to Ivan. He had nurses and a governess who cared for him day to day, but Elena was still his mother, and she interacted with him every day, always ensuring that he was cared for properly. Her main goal, however, was to ensure that Ivan did inherit the throne that his father left him.

Vasili's two troublesome brothers were still around, and even though the late grand prince had succeeded in producing two sons before his death, they were determined to claw the throne out of his grasp somehow. Vasili had known that this would happen because of how young Ivan still was, and so, as he was dying, he transferred his throne not to his tiny son but to his young wife. She was to act as regent until Ivan was old enough to take the throne.

While not unheard of, it was fairly unusual for a woman to be a regent at the time. Elena found herself possessing far more power than most noble women could even dream of, and the boyars and Ivan's uncles were circling her like vultures, determined to get their share. If Elena was less of a woman, they might have succeeded. But they weren't dealing with just some princess. Elena wasn't a girl—she was a force of nature, and she was determined to keep the throne safe until Ivan was old enough to understand the mighty responsibility that fate had placed on his small shoulders.

* * * *

Elena Glinskaya was born around 1510, the daughter of a Serbian princess and a Lithuanian duke. She was only twenty years old when Ivan was born and twenty-three when the regency fell to her, but she refused to allow her youth or gender to stop her from ruling over Moscow with a stern hand.

Immediately, Andrei of Staritsa and Yuri Ivanovich—Vasili's two brothers—started to come up with plots to have Elena deposed. They were often backed by the boyars who were none too amused with having some Lithuanian woman on the throne, but Elena defended Ivan's throne ferociously. She had Yuri thrown into prison only a year after Vasili's death; three years later, in 1537, Andrei followed, and both of them would die behind bars.

By that point, Ivan was seven years old and starting to become aware of his status as the soon-to-be grand prince. He watched as his extraordinary mother managed Moscow with aptitude and grace, unsurprising considering that she had studied politics, among other subjects, as a girl; now, she negotiated peace treaties with both Sweden and Lithuania, built a new wall around Moscow to fortify the city's defenses, and brought about a currency reform throughout Russia.

It would have been expected that Elena would merely protect the throne for a few years until Ivan could take it. Instead, she proved herself to be one of Moscow's most apt rulers, a grand princess who was far more than just a pretty face. Under her powerful influence, Ivan started his education as the young heir to the throne, and despite the fact that his father was dead, his future looked bright. With a mother like Elena Glinskaya, what could ever possibly stop him?

Meanwhile, the boyar families simmered with anger and hatred that Elena was holding onto power despite her husband's death. Two prominent families, usually involved in conflict between themselves, were particularly keen to get rid of Elena; the Shuisky and Belsky families had their sights set on the throne, and they would stop at nothing to get what they wanted.

Blissfully unaware of the trouble brewing right on his doorstep, Ivan was busy with his lessons with his governess, Agrippina Fedorovna Chelyadnina. Her first order of business was to get Ivan reading. Despite being very young and quite sensitive, the little boy quickly came to grips with the idea, and soon he was reading avidly. A widow of almost twenty years, Agrippina had been Ivan's and Yuri's governess since Vasili died, and she was a figure almost more familiar than Elena was to the boys. It was Agrippina who fed, bathed, and put them to bed, who helped them with their lessons and got them dressed in the mornings. The boys knew her as almost a second mother. Little did they know that Agrippina was part of a terrible plot—a plot that would change Ivan's young life from comfort, luxury, and education to fear, neglect, and survival.

* * * *

Agrippina slipped through the dark hallways of the castle where she lived with her two young charges and their royal mother. Clutching a tiny glass vial in her hand, she was aware of her pounding heart as she moved as light-footed as she could through the familiar building. It was snuggled safely in the heart of Moscow's Kremlin, but little did its inhabitants know that its threat came from deep within.

Nobody knows whether Agrippina was paid off for what she was about to do, if she had personal motives for her betrayal, or even if she'd been forced somehow. Perhaps she was threatened with violence; the Shuisky family was capable of anything. Either way, it is likely true that she moved through the castle on that dark night in 1538 headed on a deadly errand.

The details of that fateful day are vague and shrouded in the mists of history. One can only imagine how the morning of April 4th, 1538, must have dawned for seven-year-old Ivan. Did his governess wake and dress him like she did every morning? Had she already disappeared, and did he awaken late and sleepy to stumble half-focused to his mother's chamber? Did he find her there, cold and stiff, her body bled white of its vibrant life, her youthful eyes glassy and blank? Did he scream? Did he struggle to comprehend what was happening as he seized her cold hand, crying out for her to wake up? Did he sob as her attendants came running, and did he fight them as they dragged him away from his mother's corpse? Or perhaps Agrippina pretended that nothing was wrong. Maybe his day started like any other day until one of his mother's attendants discovered her, her scream of horror echoing throughout the entire castle. Maybe Agrippina slammed the door shut, keeping him in his nursery until some boyar could come and break the brutal truth.

Either way, with Ivan only seven years old and little Yuri not yet five, Elena Glinskaya was dead. She was probably poisoned, likely due to a plot of the Shuisky family who wanted to grab the power of the throne of Moscow for themselves. And because she had imprisoned both of their uncles (who had subsequently died in prison), Yuri and Ivan were immediately orphans.

Ivan's life took a sudden and horrific turn for the worse. His mother had been raising him to be a wise and educated ruler. But now that she was gone, Ivan's focus was on just one thing: survival.

* * * *

Elena was laid to rest in the Ascension Church, the very same one that had been built only a few years before to celebrate the birth of little Ivan. Then, he had been an innocent and uncomprehending baby, barely aware of the towering white monument that commemorated his birth. Now, still but a child, he had to watch the body of his mother disappear into that church, never to be seen again.

Ivan now found himself almost completely alone. Both his parents were dead and so were his uncles, imprisoned by his own mother. Even Agrippina, the woman who had raised him, had been arrested and tried for Elena's murder. Now, there was no one left in the world who could care for Ivan and his tiny brother. It is hard to grasp how traumatic the death of Elena must have been for the two boys, especially Yuri, who was born deaf and had also become mute.

With Elena gone and Ivan still too young to take any kind of power, the regency fell to those same arguing, petty boyars that had probably killed Elena in the first place. The Shuisky family triumphantly took the place that they had made for themselves by murderous means, although they were constantly harassed by the Belsky family, their greatest rivals.

All of Russia suffered at the hands of these selfish boyars. Their only aim was to grab money and power for themselves; governing the country and serving the people were secondary concerns. With the two families so deeply at odds, Russia found itself neglected. The boyars oppressed the common people and helped themselves to whatever treasure or money they could find, regardless of who those things truly belonged to.

Nobody, however, could have suffered more than Ivan and Yuri. Caring for the little boys fell to the Shuisky and Belsky families, and they tossed this duty to the winds. Despite the fact that he was soon to be the Grand Prince of Moscow, Ivan found himself struggling to survive and as lonely as any street urchin in his country. The prince of Russia was going to bed hungry and wearing out his clothes, neglected and despised by the strangers that had suddenly overrun his luxurious home.

Sadly, the psychological effects of this time would be disastrous, not only for Ivan, but for thousands of people.

Chapter 5 – Becoming Terrible

Even though Ivan had his blankets pulled over his head, he could hear the fighting outside his doorway. Raised voices screaming at one another, metal clashing as swords were drawn. He squeezed his eyes tight shut, knowing what was coming next. There were screams of anger and incredulity, and then there was the thin sound of metal slicing the air as the men out in the hallway slashed at one another. Steel rang on steel, grunts of effort punctuating the heavy footsteps on the floor. Then a butcher's noise, the sound of flesh ripping. There was a brief gurgle of pain before the thud of a body hit the floor. Running feet echoed in the hall as some concerned voices stayed behind until finally there was a dragging sound as the fallen man was pulled away.

Slowly, Ivan let out the breath he'd been holding. He waited for silence to fall before pushing back his blankets and sitting up in bed. Just beside him, Yuri slept, blissfully unaware that anything had happened; he lived in a silent world so at least he could sleep peacefully. Ivan, however, heard it all, those terrible sounds of the feud between the Shuisky and Belsky families that had been raging within the very palace where Ivan lived for years. The warring families' constant battles often crashed up and down the hallways; often when Ivan ventured out of his room for the first time each morning, he would see fresh bloodstains that the maids had not yet scrubbed away.

Worse, sometimes the fights spilled over into the chambers where Ivan and Yuri were playing. It was a sign of the highest disrespect for a boyar to even venture into the princes' chambers, but with no one left to advocate for the boys, the boyars did as they pleased. They fought right in front of the children, sometimes even involving the boys in their fights, harassing and molesting them as Ivan struggled to protect his deaf-mute brother. Yet what could he do? He had been just a child when the feud first started. Ever since, no one had been safe inside the Kremlin that his mother had so carefully fortified before her death; even clergymen had been stoned to death within those walls. When the Shuisky prince attempted to overthrow the Belsky prince who was then in control of the regency, they had burst into Ivan's rooms and searched it noisily. Terrified, Ivan and Yuri cowered, convinced that the Shuiskys had come to kill them at last.

It was little surprise, then, that Ivan was growing up into a strange young man. Unutterably lonely with no one to talk to who could talk back, Ivan turned to reading for companionship and solace. He read voraciously, educating himself as much as he could. Yet when he failed to understand something, his reactions could be irrational and violent; he often curled himself up on the floor and proceeded to bang his head on the cold surface, as if he could strike all the fear and pain out of himself and replace it with understanding and wisdom. He was slowly becoming an adult, but he was also already showing evidence of being profoundly disturbed.

As Ivan grew older, the boyars started to treat him with a little more respect. The people hung their hopes on the boy as being a fair grand prince someday; the Shuiskys, then in power, decided that it was easier and safer to keep him around for now than to kill him and risk an uprising. Neglect and molestation had failed to drive the young prince into madness, so as his teenage years approached, the Shuiskys decided that it would be best to simply spoil and distract him. They provided him with a string of young companions, usually noblemen about his age, and gave them all free rein to do as they pleased. Perhaps they could thus ruin Ivan and make him forget the power that was so close to slipping into his grasp.

Ivan seized upon this new opportunity for freedom with voracity. He flung himself into the same pursuit that Vasili had loved so dearly: hunting. But the steady calculation of a true huntsman was never part of Ivan's psyche. Instead, all he wanted to do was to inflict cruelty on his prey, the same cruelty that he had had to suffer for so many years as a voiceless child in the grip of the same family that had killed his mother.

Together with his reckless band of cronies, Ivan started to express his pent-up anger in terrible ways. Instead of just hunting the creatures that filled the woods surrounding Moscow, he captured and tortured them, sometimes pushing sharp objects through their eyes and sometimes casting live animals—often innocent, domestic ones, like pet dogs or cats—from the roof of the Kremlin. Pain and fear had twisted his young mind so that he enjoyed seeing others suffer. It made him feel powerful, stripping away the terrible helplessness that he had felt as a little child with nobody to protect him. And the more he behaved cruelly, the more the Shuiskys urged him on. They wanted the people to lose faith in their young prince and to see a side of him that would scare them.

As Ivan grew older, now turning twelve years old, his games started to get more and more dangerous. No longer were animals the only subject of his cruelty. With his buddies, he developed a new game to express his anger and fear. Saddling up their horses, he and his friends would gallop madly through the streets, purposely riding through the slush to spray it up against people and carts and even steering their charging steeds directly into pedestrians to knock them over and trample them.

Ivan was becoming a rogue. But he was also starting to become aware that he had more power than he'd thought at first. He wasn't just a kid cowering under the covers anymore; he had the ability to control, to hurt, and to kill. And it wouldn't be long before the young Grand Prince of Moscow performed his first execution.

* * * *

Andrei Mikhailovich Shuisky lounged in the royal rooms of the Kolomeskoye, feeling exceptionally smug and content with his life. It was easy to see why. Five years ago, he had just been another boyar, another minor noble squabbling over petty things with other men of his rank; the previous Grand Prince of Moscow had barely paid him any attention. Now, he was in control of the throne of Moscow itself. He had thoroughly lined his pockets at the expense of the royal treasury and stripped most of the palace of its furs and jewels. Even better, he was lording it over all the people of Russia. If he ever wanted something, it was his for the taking, and a little violence was enough to get whatever he wanted. He even had Grand Prince Ivan IV firmly under his control. At least, so he thought.

The door to the chamber banged open. Shuisky jumped a little, not expecting any visitors. He was shocked to see none other than Ivan himself walk inside. The young man's eyes were so dark they were almost black; they glittered with something unreadable, but there was a definite menace in the way he walked into the room. He was flanked on either side by two of the royal huntsmen, and their hands were balled into fists, looking ready for a fight.

Before Shuisky could say anything, Ivan raised his hand. His eyes were locked on Shuisky's as he pointed. "Arrest him," he ordered, his voice flat and expressionless.

The huntsmen nodded in deference to their prince and marched across to where Shuisky sat. Before he could get away, they seized him, their muscular arms effortlessly controlling him as they dragged him before the grand prince. Ivan glared at him with a contempt and hatred that burned into Shuisky's very soul. He contemplated him for a few moments, and suddenly, Shuisky felt overwhelming fear rise in his gut. The boy standing in front of him was only thirteen years old, but he seemed to tower over Shuisky at that moment like a vengeful giant, ready to destroy.

Then Ivan looked up at the huntsmen. Still just a boy, he had to tip his head quite far back to meet their eyes. "Throw him to the dogs," he said.

Shuisky screamed. He flung himself back, straining against the arms of the huntsmen, but they were only too keen to obey their grand prince and rid themselves of the oppressive regent. Ivan followed as they walked toward the enclosure where he kept his hunting dogs. There was a huge pack of them, slavering beasts with crazy eyes, fed only the bare minimum—the hungrier they were, the better they'd hunt. And they hadn't hunted for a long time. They started to bark and fling themselves against the walls as the screaming, fighting Shuisky was dragged toward their enclosure. Their white teeth flashed, drool and foam dripping from their baying jaws. The huntsmen dragged the door open, one of them beating the dogs back with a huge stick. The other seized Shuisky, and with a final scream, he was flung inside.

Immediately, the regent disappeared under a wave of hairy bodies. They fell upon him, their teeth ripping flesh, blood spraying and staining their muzzles as they fed. They didn't so much hunt him down as simply tear him apart. Fighting with each other, their teeth crunching on bones, the dogs ripped him to pieces. By the time the feeding frenzy was over, only bones remained.

And standing a little to one side, his dark eyes intent, Ivan watched it all. He had been right about his power after all, and it was intoxicating to watch as the man who had caused him so much pain was destroyed at his order. He had the power now to kill anyone who stood in his way. He would never have to suffer like he had as a small child again.

He could do whatever he wanted, have whatever he wanted. And what the young Grand Prince of Moscow wanted now, more than anything, was power.

Chapter 6 – The Coronation of the First Tsar

Illustration IV: Monomakh's Cap

The city streets echoed with the sound of thousands of church bells. The sound of them bounced from rooftop to rooftop, chasing the dawn's light across the celebrating city, as every church in Moscow tolled out its glad tidings with the pure tones of the bells filling every corner of every building. High and deep, slow or merry, the bells rang. They rang proclaiming that a new Grand Prince of Moscow was going to be crowned—and this time, he would not be simply a grand prince but also the first tsar that Russia would ever know.

Astride a shining and prancing steed, Ivan rode toward the Kremlin, his stallion tossing its head and dancing so that its iron shoes struck sparks on the street. Ivan's dark eyes glittered with anticipation. He'd been born for this day, and all of Russia had awaited his arrival with the same expectation that he felt now. Despite the best efforts of the boyars, Ivan had not only made it to manhood, but he had seized his opportunity for power.

Ever since Ivan had thrown Andrei Mikhailovich Shuisky to his hungry dogs, the Shuisky family had viewed him with fear. It was obvious that he would no longer be cowed by the warring boyars. Their days of harassing and disrespecting Ivan were over. He had finally realized how much power he had, and for a teenage boy, it was both dangerous and intoxicating.

It was three years after Shuisky's grisly death. Ivan had continued to further his education, influenced by the Metropolitan of Moscow—a man named Makari—who seems to have been one of the few positive presences in his young life. Instead of trying to grab power for himself, Makari appears to have been genuinely interested in building up a fair and able ruler over Russia. Ivan had also been studying the letters written by his grandfather, Ivan the Great, and a word in those correspondences had jumped out at him with irresistible attraction: *tsar*. Translated, the word means something like *emperor*. While the Grand Prince of Moscow was the most powerful man in Russia, considerable power was still possessed by the grand princes of other important cities all over the country. The Grand Prince of Moscow was not so much an emperor as he was the most powerful member of a group of kings. Ivan wanted to change that.

It could have been the writings of his grandfather, in which he sometimes referred to himself as "tsar" even though he did not officially bear the title, that had inspired Ivan to adopt not only the crown of the Grand Prince of Moscow but also that of Tsar of All the Russias. In doing so, Ivan proclaimed himself a descendant of Rurik, that Norse explorer who had first made Novgorod his own. He also made himself the ruler over all of the Grand Princes of Russia, unifying the government and setting himself at its very head as emperor. Word of the brutal execution of Andrei Shuisky had gotten out, and no one dared oppose him.

So, on that shining winter day of January 16th, 1547, the sixteen-year-old Ivan rode toward his coronation, ready to become the first Russian tsar. He was decked out in his princely robes which were gorgeously jeweled and ornately embroidered. The ceremony that was to follow was just as elaborate as the gleaming robes that the tsar wore. The Russian Orthodox Church presided over the entire ceremony; Makari, as the Metropolitan and thus the spiritual head of the Russian Orthodox Church, would likely have led it, reading Scripture, saying prayers, and laying his hands on young Ivan. Finally, Makari lifted the beautiful Russian crown from its place and held it out to Ivan. Known as the Monomakh's Cap, it was a striking thing wrought with gold. Today, the cap is bordered with fur and decked out in jewels, but when Ivan received it from Makari's hands, it was a plainer thing. Still gleaming in gold but lacking the trimmings, it seemed warlike, almost utilitarian. The weight in his hands was a strong reminder of the responsibility that the fate of his birthright had bestowed upon him, but Ivan could hardly wait to lift it up and rest it on his head. He was now the Tsar of All the Russias, the emperor of his world.

He was the most powerful man in the country. And he liked it.

* * * *

Before Ivan's coronation, he had realized that he needed something else in order to become a true tsar: a wife. Without being married,

Ivan would not be fully considered a man. What was more, he wouldn't be able to produce an heir, although it is possible he had a few offspring already considering there were some allegations of rape brought against him during his wild times riding through the city and causing chaos with the "friends" that the Shuiskys had prescribed for him. It was time for Ivan to find a woman, and once he had made this proclamation, nobles all over Russia immediately sprang into action.

Due to his status, Ivan would only be able to marry a woman of noble blood. In fact, it would be best for him to marry a princess— the higher her rank, the better for strengthening alliances with other powerful men in Russia. Lesser nobles, however, still tried their hand at getting their daughters to become the new tsaritsa (empress), and so hundreds of them flocked to the Kremlin to present their daughters for Ivan's inspection. By some accounts, as many as 1,500 girls were brought for Ivan to choose from.

Princess after princess was brought in and paraded like a show horse for Ivan's pleasure. He turned them all away one by one, despite their beauty and rank. The poor girls must have felt like they were cattle at some auction; it is difficult to imagine whether they were more dismayed by the insult of being turned down by the tsar-to-be or relieved not to have to spend their lives with this tempestuous young man. And the more girls Ivan turned down, the more tempestuous he became. Angry with the inferiority of the brides presented to him, Ivan grew frustrated and anxious, shouting at the girls and probably kicking a few servants around for good measure.

Then, a white-skinned, dark-eyed girl was brought forward. Mid-rant, Ivan stopped, staring at her. She was about his own age; her smooth, round cheeks were still those of a girl, but her elegant curves belonged to a woman. Her eyes were lowered, her small hands folded neatly in front of her, yet there was something a little fearless about her. Unlike the other girls, she neither groveled nor trembled. She just waited, her gaze lowered in an attitude of demure respect.

There was a stillness about her that Ivan found irresistible. He took a step closer, drinking in her sweet, soft scent. She was motionless, poised, and controlled even in her meekness. There was so much calm in her; she was a mountain lake to Ivan's stormy sea, a pure blue sky to his thundercloud, a glacier to his avalanche. She soothed something deep inside of him, and he just couldn't take his eyes off her.

Her name was Anastasia Romanovna, and she was the daughter of a minor boyar. In comparison with the other women who had been brought up for Ivan during the bride-show, she was a nobody, only a few steps above being a mere commoner. But it was neither her rank, nor her wealth, nor her beauty that attracted Ivan. It was something in her soul, something calm and resolute that tempered his madness and soothed the pain that had driven him to such unspeakable acts even at his young age.

Once Ivan met Anastasia, there was never any question about it. While he spent several weeks with his shortlist of girls to get to know them better, Anastasia was the only one who could calm him, and it didn't take long for him to fall head over heels in love with her. Only a few weeks after Ivan's coronation, they were married, and Anastasia became the tsaritsa of Russia.

Anastasia was the first bright and joyous thing in Ivan's life since the death of his mother almost ten years before. She had an undeniably positive effect on his mental state, reversing—or at least numbing—the effects that years of trauma had had on his young psyche. Her influence on him would usher in a time of justice, ambition, and capability as the first tsar—and of joy and peace in his own heart for the first time in many years.

Chapter 7 – An Ambitious Young Ruler

With Anastasia's calming influence soothing Ivan's desperate need for power, he could finally become the educated and sophisticated ruler that he always had the potential to be.

One of Ivan's key allies and advisers remained Makari, the Metropolitan of Moscow. Makari wanted the young man to govern over a united, powerful, and just land, using Christian precepts taken from the Russian Orthodox Church to set the standards for law and government. As such, as soon as he took power, Ivan began to institute a number of reforms designed to unify his scattered empire.

Most of Ivan's power was tied to the Church itself. In fact, when proclaiming himself tsar, he tightened the bonds of church and state. It is thus unsurprising that one of Ivan's first steps was to summon a series of church councils, the first of which met in 1547, the very same year of his coronation. The purpose of the councils was to organize the Church's administration, making it more systematic and methodical so that it was better suited to help Ivan deal with matters of the government. Several saints were also canonized leading to a growing list of Russian saints that included Aleksandr Nevsky, the ancestor of Ivan's who had won the fateful Battle of the Ice.

Being a young and inexperienced ruler, and not having grown up with the example and influence of his father, Ivan realized that he couldn't govern alone. Now that Anastasia was helping him to not feel so helpless and traumatized, Ivan was able to recognize his need for help and advice. To improve his government and provide himself with a platform of support and guidance, Ivan established the first *zemski sobor*.

The name translates to "assembly of the land," and essentially, it was the first parliamentary gathering in Russian history. It consisted of representatives from many different social ranks, including boyars, clergymen, monks, and even commoners as long as they were freemen and owned land. Ivan presided over these gatherings and held them often throughout his reign, usually to discuss major issues such as wars. The *zemski sobor* meetings were to become a part of the Russian government well into the seventeenth century.

With the help of these more experienced members of government, Ivan was able to put together an entirely new legal code in 1550, only three years into his reign. The previous code that Russia had been using was half a century old and had questionable roots; this one would be based, as Makari had encouraged Ivan to do, on justice and well rooted in Scripture according to the Eastern Orthodox Church. This new code was known as the Sudebnik of 1550.

Before the Sudebnik was finished, however, Ivan would face his first disaster as tsar. In the very first year of his reign, he would have to deal with the threat of almost total destruction of his seat of government. Moscow was about to endure a tragedy.

* * * *

The flames roared. They churned and charged, beaten by the wind into something that was less like a mindless natural occurrence and more like a vengeful beast that sought to destroy anything that stood in its path. Houses and streets, businesses and barns, people and animals—it didn't matter; everything was fair game to the bellowing blaze that ripped through the streets of Moscow, quicker and more destructive than any invading army.

Ivan, sixteen years old, had to watch wide-eyed from the windows of the Kremlin as the fire inched closer and closer. Most of Moscow at the time was built from wood, and every house the fire reached was nothing but fuel. Whole streets were engulfed in flames in a matter of seconds, the day turned black by the smoke that reached out its sinuous tendrils to strangle the sun. As Ivan watched, there was a terrible crack, like the sound of an enemy cannon. Everywhere, fleeing residents of the city fell flat, and Ivan himself cringed, clinging to the windowsill, but there was no enemy except for the fire itself. It had reached an armory somewhere and found a barrel of gunpowder, and the white smoke of the explosion bloomed into the air.

The streets were filled with a stampede of panicking people. Peasants and nobles, slaves and masters—there was no rank here, nothing but fear as they ran from the burning flames. Thousands of people flooded through the city as they fled, rushing over one another, trampling one another, and clinging to children and what possessions they had managed to snatch from the teeth of the blaze. The snapping and hissing of the fire were punctuated by the screams of those who had not been lucky enough. Agonized animal sounds of terror and pain rose into the sky as people were trapped and burned to death in the pitiless flames.

The heat of the fire was such that stone cracked and metal melted. Hot copper, glowing red, streamed down the walls of the houses; there were screams of pain where it dripped on people, searing through clothes and eating into human flesh. The smell was appalling, and the smoke was so thick that it was almost impossible to breathe, but the smell was worse with the odor of scalded flesh, some of it belonging to animals but much of it belonging to people as they burned and died, permeating the air. And still, the fire marched on, leaping from house to house, stalking through the city like a lion on the hunt.

The fire had no respect for the ranks of those whose homes it decimated. In that maze of wooden dwellings, with narrow and twisting alleyways, even a modern-day fire service would have found it almost impossible to contain; without hoses, fire trucks, fire hydrants, or an organized water system, the citizens of Moscow didn't stand a chance. Ivan could do little more than watch as the ravaging beast stalked closer and closer to the Kremlin.

Smoke filled the air of the Cathedral of the Dormition deep within the Kremlin, sinking into the lungs of Makari where he knelt in desperate prayer for his city. He refused to budge even after most of the other people in the cathedral had fled. Eventually, some of the clergymen had to drag him out of the building, hoisting him down to a breach in the walls of the Kremlin to lower him to the riverbank by means of a rope. Ivan and Anastasia were likely busy evacuating themselves, rushing from the fortress that would withstand any army but not the force of nature that was reducing the capital of Russia to ashes. Makari, however, still resisted; he wanted to go back to the cathedral to hold onto his silent and despairing vigil. He would have resisted more if he'd known that his companions' plan to safely lower him to the riverbank was botched. Someone's hand slipped, or perhaps the rope snapped, or maybe they just fumbled in their haste and panic. Either way, Makari tumbled to the ground, hitting the riverbank with a flat and frightening thump. They had to carry him to safety, his heart barely beating inside a broken body.

As for Ivan, he could only look back on a blazing city as thousands of people perished in the blaze, hoping that his own home might survive the onslaught of flame. He was one of the few lucky ones. The Kremlin, though blackened by smoke, was not destroyed. But by the time the fire finally died down in the small hours of June 22nd, 1547, 80,000 of Ivan's subjects would find out that they had not been so lucky. Only two-thirds of Moscow's buildings still stood, many of them damaged and sullied by the smoke; the rest were nothing but ash and rubble. By some estimates, as many as 3,700 people were dead. Children were not included in this count, so one can only speculate on how many people perished that day in the most brutal manner, burned to death in their own homes and businesses.

Ivan and Anastasia had fled to Sparrow Hills, an area on the edge of Moscow. They sought refuge there from the fire and remained safe from its awful power, but Ivan's trouble wasn't over. With 80,000 people rendered homeless, the lower classes were desperate, scared, and looking for someone to blame. That someone became Ana Glinskaya, Ivan's grandmother who was accused of using sorcery to burn down Moscow. She had seemed suspect to the peasantry ever since she had failed to hold together her daughter's regency after Elena died. Crowds formed in the streets, people with sooty faces and singed hair, their eyebrows burned from their very faces, blisters on their hands, and their voices hoarse and harsh from smoke inhalation. With blackened lips and wide, white eyes, they stormed Sparrow Hills, shouting for what they perceived to be justice. Ivan found himself helplessly pinned in his house, stripped of the fortifications that had made the Kremlin a safe residence. He had to face the screaming crowds with little to offer them. He was just sixteen years old and only six months into his reign, and already his people were rebelling against him because of something completely out of his control.

The crowds were baying for his grandmother's blood, demanding that Ivan should hand her over to him. It would have been so easy for the young ruler to panic and revert to his wild and crazy ways, perhaps to send an army to crush the desperate people or to ride out and butcher them himself the way he had galloped through the streets and knocked over pedestrians only a few years ago. But he was not the boy that he had been then. He was a rational and steady man thanks to the presence of the sweet and gentle Anastasia by his side. She calmed him, soothed him, and allowed him to think straight. And so, instead of panicking, Ivan negotiated. He refused to hand over his grandmother but succeeded in defusing the crowd with promises of laws that would prevent this from ever happening again. Shortly afterward, Ivan made good on his promise. He made it a law for every residence to have a water barrel on its rooftop, another in its garden, and for cooking stoves to be kept far from residential buildings. These precautions were a huge step forward toward protecting Moscow from fire, although in the later years of Ivan's reign, they would prove to not be enough. He also made some changes in the administration that allowed members of the lower classes to hold somewhat more power in lower positions of the government.

Ivan had weathered the first great storm of his reign, and he had done so admirably, negotiating a peaceful resolution to what could have been a bloody rebellion and taking significant steps toward preventing such a tragedy from ever occurring again. While he was left with a ravaged city and faced the monumental task of rebuilding Moscow, Ivan's future was looking bright. And for the next few years, his reign would only get brighter.

Chapter 8 – Books and Cathedrals

Illustration V: St. Basil's Cathedral, modern day

Even while he was trying to rebuild Moscow, Ivan's attention was soon demanded on the more distant front of the Volga River.

Five hundred miles away from the ashes of Ivan's capital city, there stood the city of Kazan. It was a glittering shard from the shattered pieces of the Golden Horde, the great Mongolian kingdom that had once commanded the length and breadth of Russia. Ivan the Great had freed his country from their tyranny, but he had failed to conquer Kazan. It remained as the last stronghold of that once great power and a brooding menace on the border of Russia. Kazan controlled the Volga River, an important trade route, preventing Russia from engaging in trade with Siberia and other areas. Worse, the people of Kazan conducted frequent raids into Russia itself, looting towns for their treasures and even kidnapping Russians to sell to the Persian and Turkish slave markets.

Something would have to be done about Kazan. And the moment that Ivan took power, he decided that the time had come to do it. Ignoring the problem would not only result in Russia's continued inability to trade along the Volga, but Ivan feared that the Tatars of Kazan might even invade; given time and space to grow their army, they could even return to the former glory of the Golden Horde and wreak just as much havoc as their ancestors had. Ivan was determined to follow in his grandfather's footsteps and rid Russia of the Tatars once and for all.

The same year that he was made tsar, Ivan sent a campaigning army out to Kazan in a bid to bring the last of the Tatars to their knees. He also ordered the fortress of Svyazhsk to be built on the banks of the Volga opposite Kazan; it was designed upriver by the best of Russia's architects, and the pieces of the fortress were even built there, being floated down to the front in numbered bits like a prefab house.

Still, for three years, the Russians struggled with the Tatars, never gaining any ground and never winning any major battles. Svyazhsk was built, the army went to battle, yet it was to no avail. By 1552, Ivan—then in his early twenties—had sent out two different campaigns against Kazan, but the fortress of his enemies remained stubbornly in place, defying his authority as Tsar of All the Russias. So, Ivan finally decided that he would have to lead his army himself.

He kissed Anastasia goodbye, leaving her behind in the safety of the Kremlin, and rode out to war.

The past five years had been the golden era of Ivan's reign with many reforms in the government, including many that limited the power of the hated boyars that had made Ivan's childhood so unutterably miserable. Personally, however, for Ivan himself, there had been deeply difficult times. Anastasia had borne him their first child in 1548, a little girl who so closely resembled her mother that they named her Anna. She enjoyed all the happiness that Ivan had been denied as a child. Even though Ivan was only eighteen at the time, with Anastasia even younger, this was not an unusual age to become parents during that era. Little Anna would have had excellent care from her experienced nurses as well as her parents. But sadly, regardless of the care they received, medieval children were still playing a dangerous game of survival simply by being alive. With child mortality rates in the Middle Ages soaring as high as fifty percent, all children had a slim chance of making it to adulthood, mostly due to the poor medical practices that allowed many childhood diseases to run rampant. Poor little Anna likely succumbed to one of these, passing away in 1550, less than a month before her second birthday.

Less than a year after the death of Anna, Anastasia gave birth to another little girl. This one, named Maria, was born on March 17th, 1551. While her date of death is unknown, Maria would not live long either. She was possibly still alive when her father left for Kazan in 1552.

Still, Ivan and Anastasia were both young, and he knew that more children would come. He had Anastasia, so he felt that nothing could really stand against him as her loving presence gave him the security that he hadn't been able to cling to since the death of his mother, Elena. Now, he rode confidently for Kazan, determined to subdue it at last.

It was the summer of 1552, and Ivan was almost twenty-two years old, but he was at the head of a tremendous army. 150,000 strong, it consisted of infantry, cavalry, and even the heavy artillery that would be necessary to bring down the strong stone walls of Kazan. Ivan had tried to negotiate with the Khan of Kazan, but all attempts to find a peaceful resolution had failed. Finally, Ivan had threatened the khan with war, turning it into a conflict of religions as Eastern Orthodox Russia met Muslim Kazan. The khan was arrogant in his response. "All is ready for you here," he told the young tsar contemptuously. "We invite you to the feast."

And so, on August 30th, 1552, Ivan and his army pitched their tents on the banks of the Volga, determined to take Kazan. While Ivan was with the army, it was primarily led by more experienced military commanders, among them Ivan's close friend Andrei Mikhailovich Kurbsky.

At once, they dragged forth the most intimidating weapons they had in their arsenal: cannons. These majestic weapons could cause an awe-inspiring amount of carnage, spewing heavy projectiles across vast distances to crush opposing soldiers and destroy whole sections of castle walls. It was in bucketing rain and with several cannons that Ivan opened his attack on Kazan, hammering the walls with cannonballs that punched through the wood. Yet somehow those walls seemed impenetrable despite the destruction sown by Ivan's cannons. The Tatars were quick to repair their broken fortifications, swarming over the walls of their fortress and holding it up against the deadly onslaught.

Through the driving rain, Ivan ordered his infantry forward. Blinking and struggling against the wind, they charged, but they were effortlessly repulsed. Worse, when they staggered back to camp, they found that their tents were flapping uselessly in the wind; everything was soaked, and the gunpowder that drove Ivan's cannons was under threat by the storm.

Ivan could think of only one explanation for the terrible weather. The people of Kazan, viewed by the Russians as being devilish pagans, were casting some kind of a curse on his army. They must have commanded the storm to stop their enemies. He ordered a religious relic to be brought to the battlefield, and legend has it that the storm stopped at once.

Now, Ivan's men could renew their attack, and they did so with vigor and zeal, spurred on by the hope that divine powers were on their tsar's side. Undermining the Tatars' defenses, the Russians started to at last bring down some of the walls of Kazan. A breakthrough came several weeks into the siege when Ivan's men succeeded in blowing up Kazan's water system, rendering the citizens helpless and their situation suddenly desperate. Without water, the city could not hold out against Ivan's might.

Still, the defenders clung on grimly, knowing that laying down their arms now would likely mean that most of them would be butchered anyway—such was siege warfare of the Middle Ages. Ivan, on his knees and praying desperately for victory, thought of a new tactic. He had some of his Tatar prisoners brought out and led to where they were within sight of the defenders, ordering them—probably by force—to beg their people to surrender and be done with it. As the prisoners' terrified voices rose into the air, a rain of arrows rose to meet them. The defenders shot down their own people where they stood in bonds among Ivan's soldiers.

Their brutal defiance proved to be fruitless. On October 2nd, 1552, Ivan gazed out over the beleaguered city and knew that he had as good as won already. He gave the order, and his army rushed forward, a wave of infantry slamming against the gates of Kazan. Ivan remained back in the camp, praying for a victory in his first campaign as tsar. And as he waited, the walls of Kazan fell at last. The people within were put to the sword, and Ivan made no move to stop his bloodthirsty hordes from butchering everything in their path. Hundreds had already died in the siege, and hundreds more died that day as the Russians at last could vent their fury on their stubborn and tenacious foe.

* * * *

Kazan was practically razed to the ground. The Russian forces overran the city, and their victory was as decisive as it was complete, leaving Ivan in total control of Kazan and the Middle Volga. His victory opened up the trade route that he'd been desperately hoping to control, and Ivan rode back to Moscow to be given a hero's welcome, as well as glad news. Anastasia had borne Ivan his third child, and this time, it was a little boy. Ivan would not be faced with the same struggle that his father had. The little boy was named Dmitri.

To celebrate his annexation of Kazan, Ivan ordered the building of one of Russia's most famous churches: St. Basil's Cathedral. This towering work of art, a majestic thing of graceful curves and glittering color, was completed in 1554. It has since become a landmark of Moscow; set at the very center of the famous Red Square, the cathedral is now painted in dazzling colors with bright designs on its patterned roofs. When Ivan ordered for it to be built, however, it was a study of elegance in white stone, its roof clad in blinding gold. It was designed to match the Kremlin, and its beauty was unrivaled—so much so that a legend exists claiming that Ivan had its architect brutally blinded so that he could never build something that would be the equal of it. This, however, has proven to be nothing more than a myth.

The truth is that as St. Basil's Cathedral took shape on Ivan's doorstep, he had not yet earned his moniker of Ivan the Terrible. The cruelty that had shaped his boyhood was still hidden, sung to sleep by the lullaby of Anastasia's presence. With baby Dmitri in her arms, she remained a safe harbor for Ivan's stormy soul.

For the next seven years, his rule continued in relative peace and success. In 1553, the year after Kazan fell, Ivan ordered the introduction of Russia's first printing press. The Moscow Print Yard was its home, a stately, palace-like building in the heart of Moscow. The elegant white pillars and extravagant halls of the Print Yard now house a university, but during Ivan's reign, multiple books were printed there in Russian and distributed throughout the country. It was a breakthrough in literature and education, and it was Ivan's attempt to pay back the only companions he had had in his dark and troubled childhood—books and reading.

By 1556, Ivan had relatively peacefully annexed Astrakhan, another enemy city farther along the Volga. He now had complete control over the trade routes to Siberia. Slave markets were destroyed, and while thousands of Muslims were displaced to make room for Ivan's Eastern Orthodox citizens, the annexation of this khanate opened up cultural borders for Russia.

It was all going well for the young tsar. For the first time in his life, he had control and comfort, along with a secure young family, a burgeoning country, and people who were loyal to their first steady ruler since the death of Vasili. The future was looking bright for Ivan, and his cruel and strange ways seemed to have been left behind somewhere in the shadows of his unhappy past.

Little did he know that his life—and the fate of all Russia—was about to take an appalling turn for the worse.

Chapter 9 – Death in the Family

Illustration VI: A mixed media figurine of Tsaritsa Anastasia Romanovna by George S. Stuart, photographed by Peter d'Aprix.

Ivan feared he was on his deathbed.

Quaking with weakness, his burning skin dry and chafing against his bedclothes, Ivan could barely make out the shape of the ceiling above him. Fever dreams chased one another through his mind and into his reality, bringing back flashes of his terrible past. Vague flickers of his father's face fading into images of his mother. The sound of her laughter. Her smell. The screams when they found her, cold and lifeless, poisoned by the boyars. Ivan tossed in his bed, his black hair soaked with sweat as he moaned against the dreams which just kept coming. Clinging to Yuri in abject terror as the boyars fought outside their bedroom chambers, hungry and scared and alone. Riding through the streets of Moscow, trampling all in his path. The strange satisfaction he found in hurting others. The shrieks of Andrei Shuisky as the hunting hounds tore him limb from limb. Ivan's coronation as tsar. Anastasia…

Anastasia. Ivan opened his eyes. Anastasia was leaning over him, her beautiful face lined with worry. She laid a cool hand against his blazing forehead, and he could see the concern in her eyes. Ivan's physicians had told him that the illness he had could not be cured. Even though he was just twenty-three years old, he was going to die young.

The fact that Ivan had a son and heir—Dmitri, then only a few months old—was little comfort to him. Vasili also had an heir when he died, but because Ivan was so young, all of Russia was still plunged into chaos and darkness as the boyars grappled for power. Ivan knew that he couldn't allow the same thing to happen. Even though his reforms had stripped the boyars of much of their power, there was nothing to prevent them from seizing the country that Ivan had so carefully cultivated and ripping it apart in their slavering jaws—just like Ivan's dogs had torn Andrei Shuisky limb from limb.

Ivan was desperate. He couldn't let that happen to his Russia, and he couldn't condemn his beloved wife to the struggle that Elena had to face in her final years, much less allow Dmitri to suffer the childhood that he had endured. Fully believing that he was dying, he sent out messages to all of the boyars, demanding that they swear their unconditional allegiance to baby Dmitri.

The boyars, too, knew that he was dying. And as one man, they refused.

* * * *

Despite what his physicians had said, however, Ivan didn't die. He recovered, although something in his mind was never the same again. It was as if the fever had stripped away some of the joy and peace that Anastasia had brought to his psyche, once again revealing the raw pain and agonized cruelty that had characterized him as a boy. Some historians speculate that the physiological effects of the illness—the nature of which is still uncertain—led to his declining mental health. However, the refusal of the boyars to accept little Dmitri as their ruler could have been equally to blame. The hated boyars that had made Ivan's childhood so unutterably miserable had now committed what he saw as a terrible act of treason, and Ivan couldn't forgive them.

Even if the boyars had agreed to swear allegiance to Dmitri, it would ultimately have mattered little. Just a few months after his father's miraculous recovery, little Dmitri squirmed out of the arms of his nurse and fell to the ground as she was walking around the grounds of the Kremlin with him. Before she could catch him, the toddler splashed into the river. Not yet one year old, the little tsarevich drowned.

Despite the boyars' betrayal and Dmitri's death, it would seem that Ivan managed to more or less pick up the pieces and cope—or perhaps it was Anastasia who was able to put his injured soul back together after every blow. She stayed steadfastly by his side throughout it all, and after his recovery, Ivan seemed to return to his normal self for a while and turned back to campaigning and conquests.

Once both Kazan and Astrakhan had been captured, Ivan set his sights still farther afield: Livonia. Comprised of lands that today are part of Latvia and Estonia, Livonia was a country bordering Russia, blocking the passage of Russian merchants to the Baltic Sea. Keen to open up another trade route, Ivan decided to launch a campaign to invade Livonia and capture it to expand Russia's territory. In 1558, he started the Livonian War, a conflict that was to continue for many years.

The precarious balance of the tsar's fragile mental state had wobbled but returned to normal. Yet it would not remain that way for long. A tragedy was about to strike—one that, even after the deaths of both his parents and losing several children, would prove to be too much for Ivan the Terrible to handle.

* * * *

As the summer of 1560 brought a blush of green to the cheeks of the countryside surrounding Moscow, Ivan gazed out of the windows of the Kremlin, contentedly studying the city over which he ruled. It was beautiful and bustling; the glittering golden roofs of his new cathedral caught the sun, reminding him of his resounding victory over Kazan. Having heard glad news from the Livonian front where his men had successfully overrun many of the Livonian knights according to Andrei Mikhailovich Kurbsky, the same commander that had helped lead Ivan's army to victory at Kazan, Ivan hoped that another great victory was at his fingertips.

As for his home life, things were looking up. Anastasia remained in the bloom of health and had given birth to three more children since the death of little Dmitri: another boy, Ivan, in 1554; a daughter named Eudoxia in 1556; and a third son, Feodor, in 1557. Little Eudoxia only survived eighteen months, joining Ivan's first three children in the royal tombs. But Ivan Ivanovich and Feodor were both healthy and strong. Ivan was particularly proud of his eldest son, who had now just turned six. He was a sprightly boy, intelligent, and being given everything that Ivan himself had been denied as a child. Ivan was determined to give his son the best start possible—after all, he would be tsar one day.

Ivan smiled to himself as he looked out over the city. He could never have asked for a better tsaritsa than his beloved Anastasia. She was as beautiful as she was gentle and had borne him healthy, vigorous children. Evidence would suggest, too, that Anastasia's love for Ivan was genuine and fervent. She loved him not only because of how well he ruled during their marriage but also because of how much he cared for her. And he couldn't have cared for her more than on that summer's day in 1560 when Tsaritsa Anastasia Romanova became suddenly and inexplicably sick. Ivan rushed to her bedside to find his young wife, who had been so healthy only a few days before, a mere ghost of herself. Her thoughts and words were scrambled; normally so patient, now her moods swung wildly, and her hands shook uncontrollably.

At once, all of the best physicians in the city were summoned and ordered to save the tsaritsa. Driven on by the wild cries of Ivan, they did everything they could for Anastasia. But as the days then weeks passed, she didn't get any better—she got worse. Sweat soaked her brown hair, pinning it down to her pillow as she gasped and thrashed on her luxurious bed. Her flawless face was pale, her clothes stained with sweat and vomit, and her breath came in ragged and rattling gasps as her muscles struggled and failed to perform their everyday functions. Her limbs twitched uncontrollably, and as Ivan stared into her dark eyes and implored her to come back to him, it seemed that she could no longer recognize him or perhaps no longer see—he couldn't tell which.

Ivan screamed; he beat the walls with his fists, he shouted, he raged, he prayed, and he begged for his beautiful wife to live. But Anastasia was too far gone. On August 7th, 1560, at the age of only thirty years old, she breathed her last. The sweet young soul that had tempered the madness of Russia's supreme ruler had left the world.

To say that Ivan was devastated would be a disgusting understatement. He was not merely heartbroken—it was more as if the death of Anastasia had reached into his chest and ripped his heart clean out, leaving only an aching and empty hole. Her death didn't wound him; it destroyed him. The man that he had become as her husband—the man that he might have been all along if his childhood had not been such an ordeal—was gone, shattered, torn apart by his inconsolable loss. In the face of such insurmountable grief, Ivan seemed to have simply lost his mind. He threw himself onto the floor of his fortress and banged his head over and over again on the marble until his blood ran and smeared, and still he went on, trying to hammer the agony out of himself. Anastasia was the only one who had ever been able to handle him in his rages; now, there was nobody, and Ivan's two little sons could only have listened as their father mutilated himself in his terrible pain.

Anastasia was laid to rest in the Ascension Convent in the Kolomenskoye, not far from the church of that same name built to honor the birth of Ivan himself. The two little boys were now motherless, and their father was driven wild by grief. In the following months, Ivan would go on a rampage of torture and execution, convinced that Anastasia had been poisoned by one of the hated boyars. They had betrayed him when he was ill, they had hated him as a child, and now he was sure that they had killed the one thing that could soothe his injured heart. Whether or not the boyars did kill Anastasia is still uncertain, but historians have since uncovered evidence that strongly suggests that Anastasia was poisoned by mercury. There is no way of knowing who exactly poisoned her, but Ivan was too deep in the throes of his bereavement to care. He tortured and killed anyone whom he was even vaguely suspicious of, seeking solace once more in hurting those weaker than him now that Anastasia was no longer there for him.

Sadly, this was only the beginning. Ivan's reign and personal life would go into a terrible tailspin following Anastasia's death. And the boyars, whether they were involved in any crimes or not, were about to pay for everything their families had ever done to him.

Chapter 10 – Betrayal

With Anastasia gone, Ivan only had one friend left to him in all the world. While the Russian populace adored him—with the obvious exception of the boyars—Ivan had never seemed capable of forming close ties with anyone apart from his wife and his single close friend: Andrei Mikhailovich Kurbsky.

Kurbsky had been a part of Ivan's reign from the very beginning, helping him in his first military campaign against Kazan and now fighting in Livonia. When Anastasia died, it was natural that Kurbsky would reach out to his friend and try to bring him some form of comfort and solace. But as Ivan continued to wreak havoc through the ranks of the boyars, harming and killing them left and right, Kurbsky started to back away from his old friend. Although Kurbsky himself appears to have been a fairly just and rational man, he was a boyar himself, and he'd personally known, and even been related to, many of the people that Ivan was treating so mercilessly. Kurbsky wanted Anastasia's killer to be punished, as did all of Russia, but he knew that Ivan was not acting for justice. He was acting for some way of expressing and relieving the incredible pain that he was feeling.

Perhaps Kurbsky tried to talk sense into Ivan. Maybe he even tried to stop him. But Ivan was having none of it. His pain was incoherent and overwhelming, and he had the power to deal with it any way he wanted—even if that meant taking innocent lives.

Kurbsky had been fighting Ivan's wars for decades, and he was starting to grow weary of his moody ruler. So, he began to pull away from him, slowly distancing himself from the tempestuous tsar.

* * * *

It could easily have been expected that Ivan would not remarry, not after the death of the one person in the world whom he had truly loved. But whether it was political pressure, the hope of giving his boys a stepmother, or just a desperate longing for companionship that prompted him to do so, Ivan started seeking for another wife almost before Anastasia's body was cold.

The hunt for a suitable bride for the Tsar of All the Russias began, but this time it was not in the same festive mood that had brought about the bride-show thirteen years ago when Ivan had fallen in genuine love with the young daughter of a minor noble. Ivan's heart was gone now, torn away by Anastasia's death. Now he was seeking a wife for her looks, wealth, or power. And Maria Temryukovna was all of the above.

The daughter of the Muslim prince of Kabarda, a part of the Caucasian region, Maria was a striking and priceless beauty. She turned heads everywhere she went with her smooth complexion and bright eyes, and what was more, their marriage was of strategic and symbolic importance. The Caucasus bordered on Russia, and even though the Livonian War was still in progress, Ivan was always keeping an eye out for a way to further expand his territory. The Caucasus was a logical next step, and marrying into its nobility was a logical first step. Ivan was captured by Maria's looks, but he was persuaded by her lineage, and they were married in 1561.

All of Russia had adored Anastasia. She had given them a stable and sensible ruler who had been able to improve the lives of many people. But Maria—she was another story. Beauty or not, she was, firstly, a pagan in their eyes. Although she converted to the Orthodox Church to marry Ivan, she was still viewed as being a foreigner of a foreign religion, and it didn't help that Anastasia's last request to Ivan had been to ask him not to marry a pagan woman. His marriage of Maria went directly against Anastasia's wishes.

To make matters worse, Maria's temperament was as far removed from Anastasia's as could be imagined. Where Anastasia had been wise, devout, gentle, and adept at controlling her husband's wild mood swings, Maria was vain and shallow. She failed to attend to her responsibilities as stepmother to Ivan Ivanovich and Feodor, and, worse, she was practically illiterate. The couple didn't get along on any level, and she became progressively less and less popular with the people.

Two years of marriage dragged past, and finally, in 1563, Maria gave birth to her first child. It was a little boy, and Ivan named him Vasili after his father, pleased that he now had three young sons to care for Russia when he was gone. Vasili, however, died when he was less than two months old, and Maria would never again bear children.

Ivan was once again keenly experiencing that isolation that had plagued him as a little orphan in the Kremlin when his only companion had been his deaf and mute little brother. Now, even Yuri was no longer at Ivan's side; even though Ivan had provided him with everything he could have possibly needed, he died of natural causes in 1563. He was closely followed by the Metropolitan Makari, who had never fully recovered from the injuries he received when he fell during the Great Fire of 1547. He had been one of Ivan's staunchest supporters, and he passed away peacefully in 1563.

And so, ransacked by grief, tortured by his past, drained by constant paranoia, and feeling utterly alone, the emperor wandered the halls of the Kremlin, a ship tossed on stormy waters, his anchor stripped away by the cruel elements. The atrocities that Ivan had committed and would yet commit have led historians to label him as a psychopath, yet looking into the tragic circumstances of his lonely existence, it's an unlikely guess.

The trouble wasn't that Ivan didn't have any feelings. It was that he had too many.

* * * *

By 1564, Ivan had taken little action when it came to the administration of his country since Anastasia's death. Gripped by his fear and loneliness, he had more or less just kept Russia running; the war in Livonia plodded on with little real progress for either side.

This frustrated Kurbsky endlessly. While Ivan hung about listlessly in the Kremlin, Kurbsky was on the front lines, watching his men die. Russia's lack of progress was costing thousands of lives in the fighting, and Kurbsky had to do something about it. He was afraid, too, for his life and for the lives of his family; so many of the boyars had already been killed following Anastasia's death, and Kurbsky wasn't sure if Ivan's paranoia had any boundaries.

By contrast, Ivan's opponent, King Sigismund II of Poland, was an able and experienced ruler who had succeeded in uniting Poland, Lithuania, and Livonia into one powerful kingdom. He was capable, strong, and active in expanding and strengthening his kingdom. Kurbsky felt that he would be safer and more successful serving Sigismund rather than the unstable tsar who had once been his close friend, and so, he defected to the Livonian side, going to Sigismund to offer him his services as a military commander. Knowing that Kurbsky was one of Moscow's best, Sigismund gladly accepted him into his service and put him to work fighting against the very men that he had once commanded.

For Ivan, Kurbsky's defection was a complete and utter blindside. Kurbsky had been the one boyar that Ivan felt he could trust; that was why he had made his old friend the commander of his forces in Livonia in a time when he was incapable of thinking straight. Now, the last pillar that Ivan had left to lean on was yanked cruelly out from under him. He responded the only way that he knew how—in rage and terror. Seizing Kurbsky's lands, he proceeded to persecute his family, writing furious letters to Kurbsky to condemn him for what he had done. Kurbsky, however, was firm in his decision. He was going to serve Sigismund now. Ivan could throw all the temper tantrums he wanted; they weren't going to change his mind.

In Ivan's eyes, Kurbsky's actions were the highest form of treason from one of the only people left in the world that he felt he could trust. Now, he realized that he couldn't trust anyone. His wife and mother had both been poisoned right in front of his eyes, killed by the boyars, and now his best friend had joined his enemy in trying to destroy him. Ivan was alone, and he was scared to death. He knew that he wasn't untouchable, and even though the people liked him and were loyal to him, the boyars both disliked and distrusted him.

Ivan felt like a little child again. He wore the title of tsar, yet at any moment, his own boyars could turn against him. Would they kill him like they killed Anastasia and Elena? He didn't want to give them the chance. And so, in secret, Ivan slipped out of Moscow.

He could think of only one place where he would feel safe: Aleksandrovskaya Sloboda. The hunting lodge was secreted away in the deep woods a few days' ride north of Moscow. It was isolated, yet strong and defensible, and had likely been a favorite haunt of his father Vasili before his death. Vasili had stayed there during his happy hunting trips, but Ivan fled there in fear now, looking over his shoulder as he rode, accompanied only by a small retinue in whom he tentatively placed a little trust. It was winter, and the falling snow masked the hoofprints of the horses, covering the icy landscape around them in a blanket of white.

When the tsar's absence was noted in the Kremlin, little was thought of it at first. It was not uncommon for the tsar to go on hunting expeditions; besides, he remained a pious and churchgoing man, and it would not have been unusual for him to have also ridden out on a pilgrimage. But as the days passed, the people began to worry. Where had Ivan gone? And why had he kept his movements so secret?

On January 3rd, 1565, the answers to their questions came in the form of two letters from Ivan. The first was addressed to the boyars, and it did not mince words. In it, Ivan confessed that he was afraid for his life and that he could no longer tolerate the treachery that he had been embroiled in ever since he was a little child. It also announced his intention to abdicate the throne. The power that being Tsar of All the Russias had given him was no longer more important to him than staying alive. He wanted to leave it all behind, all the intrigue and the danger and everything that had broken him, everything that had destroyed him to the point where he now was, and stay in his hunting lodge in the woods with only a handful of trusted servants.

In the second letter, Ivan addressed his people directly. He reassured them that he had been honored to be their tsar and that the boyars were the only reason why he felt he had no option but to abdicate. Whether this was a genuine apology or a clever ploy of Ivan's is uncertain, but either way, it was certainly advantageous to Ivan's position. Enraged at the boyars for taking away their source of trust and stability in the government, the common people turned on them, threatening violence and revolt. The boyars themselves realized that the time when Ivan had been a child and the regency had been split among them had not been a good time for them either. Many boyars had been killed as they struggled between themselves, and none of them had ever truly risen to the power of the regency. The boyars realized that if Ivan did abdicate, then not only would the commoners be likely to engage in a violent uprising, but there would be no unified government to deal with them. Moscow and all of Russia was likely to find itself embroiled in utter chaos.

Waiting for a response to the letters, Ivan roamed through his lodge, enjoying all of the luxuries that he was used to back in the Kremlin. He spent much of his time in his enormous library where he had amassed a vast collection of books, some of them incredibly old and rare even then. Ivan was on the very brink of losing everything, but perhaps here in this time when his title as tsar hung in the balance, we may find one rare moment where Ivan's heart was at peace. He was alone, but at least he was safe. One is left to wonder if the tsar's story would have had a happier ending if he had stayed in Aleksandrovskaya Sloboda with his books for the rest of his life as he'd intended.

Yet it was not to be. The boyars were shocked by Ivan's abdication, and they realized that Russia needed him, temperamental as he was. They begged him to return, and Ivan was reluctant at first. As much as he had enjoyed being tsar, he couldn't bear the thought of ever being betrayed again. The boyars kept pleading him to come back, and eventually, Ivan relented, but on one terrible condition: He wanted free rein to persecute traitors any way that he liked, avoiding all legal channels. Such was their desperation that the boyars agreed.

Ivan returned, and order was restored to Moscow. The first Tsar of All the Russias would continue to hold onto his crown. But the boyars would learn to regret their decision. They were about to enter an age of terror and darkness the likes of which they had never seen before.

Chapter 11 – Revenge

Illustration VII: Ivan IV and Maluta Skuratov *by G. Sedov. Skuratov is recorded as being a senior officer of the* Oprichniki.

Upon his return to Moscow, Ivan found himself confronted with the most challenges he had ever faced as tsar. Kurbsky's defection had led to a massive turn for the worse in the Livonian War with the Russian forces struggling without their strongest leader; the war had been raging for years now and was starting to take its toll on Russia's money and manpower. Knowing this, the Tatars started small invasions on Russia's borders, trying to take advantage of this new weakness to bring down the juggernaut that had so easily captured Kazan and Astrakhan in the 1550s. Also linked to the Livonian War was sea trading blockages put up by the Poles and Swedes in an attempt to cripple Russia's economy by denying the nation access to sea trade routes. Famine and drought started to plague the country, and for the first time since his ascension to the throne, Ivan's common people were experiencing nationwide hunger.

If he had still been in the peaceful and intelligent frame of mind with which he had governed Russia during his early rule, Ivan might have addressed these issues. He might have been able to overcome them and restore Russia to the glory of the previous decade. But Ivan was fixated on just one thing, and that was the treachery that the boyars had committed against him. They had made his childhood a living hell and taken away from him the two women that he had truly loved—and now they had given him on a silver platter all the power he needed to pay those cruelties back. He now had the power they had over him when he was a helpless little boy being molested and terrified in his own home.

Ivan started by dividing Russia into two different states: the *Zemshchina* and the *Oprichnina*. The *Zemshchina* was the majority of Russia, ruled over by the boyars under Ivan as it had always been, but the *Oprichnina* was a separate territory, mostly in the northern part of Russia, and within that territory, the boyars had no power. Ivan had absolute control over everything that happened within the *Oprichnina*, and he all but withdrew completely from governing—or even setting foot within—the *Zemshchina*. He refused to communicate with the boyars of the *Zemshchina*, abandoning them to rule the land that they had so greedily wanted and instead focused on building up a new court.

The *Oprichnina* was an unusual move and the brainchild of a mind driven wild by terror. It is universally viewed as evidence that Ivan's mental stability was questionable at best. While he may have been trying to balance out power and bring stability to Russia by forming the *Oprichnina*, it is more likely that Ivan was simply trying to be perfectly certain of his personal safety by effectively dividing his country in half: one part for the boyars and their treacherous ways and the other only for Ivan and the people he trusted, a place where nobody could poison or hurt him again.

In order to enforce the borders of the *Oprichnina* and to protect his own person, Ivan formed a new legion of guards and soldiers, something akin to the secret police of other dictatorial regimes in later centuries. Only these police were everything but secret. Known as the *Oprichniki*, they were a terrifying sight, always dressed in black and riding shining black horses. Attached to the breastplate of his horse, each *Oprichnik* carried the head of a dead dog, symbolizing his diligence in sniffing out treachery; he also wore a broom, showing that he would sweep away any opposition without effort. They were formidable warriors, hand-picked from the ranks of Russia's best for their excellence and ruthlessness in fighting (as long as they were not descended from any of the noble families), and they were fiercely loyal to Ivan—after all, they knew that the penalty for even suspected treason was torture and death. They knew this because they were the ones who carried out these penalties. Utterly loyal to Ivan's bidding, they rode all over the country, carrying out his orders to pillage, kill, maim, and torture whomever he wanted.

The *Oprichniki* themselves had a reputation for being utterly heartless. Not only did they obey Ivan's orders to carry out unmentionable cruelties, but they also had a bloodthirsty tendency themselves. Given free rein to do as they pleased, they raped and stole wherever they went, often killing innocent people for the simple sport of it. Like shadows across the landscape, they rode in their dark regiments with swift savagery, dealing out sorrow and agony everywhere they went. And with Ivan at their backs, they were untouchable and unaccountable to anyone. As long as they remained loyal to their tsar, they could do as they pleased. In Kurbsky's words, they were "children of darkness."

It was likely during this period that Ivan started to become known as Ivan the Terrible, even among his own people. For as much as Ivan himself was focused mostly on persecuting the boyars, ordering the deaths of hundreds of them, often with calculated cruelty in symbolic torture and execution rituals, he had failed to consider the effects that this would have on the common people. When the boyars suffered, they made their commoners suffer too; also, the *Oprichniki* failed to make the same distinction that Ivan did between boyars and everyone else, and they meted out the same cruelty to everyone they came across. As a result, thousands of peasants fled the *Oprichnina* and sought refuge either in the *Zemshchina* or even beyond the borders of Russia.

More of them would have fled if they had known what was coming. After five years of raining terror down upon the boyars and the rest of his people, Ivan was only getting started. His greatest atrocity was yet to come.

* * * *

Ivan's horse snorted uneasily, its huge muscles twitching under its rider as it scented the city lying ahead. Snow crunched under its hooves, steam blooming from its nostrils and curling from its sweating flanks. Ivan spurred it impatiently, keeping it moving through the deep snow. His eyes burned with a fevered paranoia, with the wild anger and hatred that had been growing inside him like a gnarled root. For years, Ivan had been suffering and inflicting that suffering upon his country. And today he would snap. He could feel it. Today he would finally let loose all of that pain and wild agony, and he would destroy, and perhaps it would make him feel somewhat better. His horse made its way over the hill, and Ivan spotted the city ahead; its sprawling mass was surrounded by his soldiers. It was now home to tens of thousands of people, a far cry from the little settlement it had once been when Rurik first made his way to Russia and gave rise to a new dynasty. To Rurik, it had been paradise. To Ivan, it was a target: Novgorod.

The five years since the creation of the *Oprichnina* and his *Oprichniki* had not been easy ones, neither for Russia nor for its tsar. As Ivan rode toward the doomed city, it was still staggering from the blow of a devastating outbreak of plague which had killed as many as 10,000 of its population. The same plague was in the middle of ravaging Moscow itself, taking a thousand lives a day and eventually killing up to one-third of the population. Bodies were heaping up in the streets, and there was nothing that could be done to stop it.

For two years, Russia had also been facing conflict with the Ottoman Empire, a massive power that Russia could not possibly hope to beat with its ruler's sanity on shaky ground and his reputation as a military commander slowly going down the drain in the wake of his failing struggles against Livonia. The Ottoman Turks were determined to dig a canal between the Volga and Don Rivers, and they had already laid siege to some Russian castles to facilitate their plans. It had taken some skillful negotiations from Ivan's diplomats to bring about a peaceful conclusion without major battles, but Russia had certainly felt the pressure of the threat from Turkey.

On the home front, life had not been easy for Ivan either. Marriage with Maria had become unbearable. Ivan Ivanovich and Feodor did not get along with her, the public was now calling her a witch, and the allure of her beauty had long since worn off in the face of her terrible conduct. Ivan was sick of her, and in his fragile mental state, it didn't take much for him to reach a tipping point that made him capable of the unthinkable. To this day, we're not sure exactly how Maria's death in 1569 came about. But it is alleged, and not impossible, that Ivan himself committed the very act of treason that had driven him so wildly insane in the first place. He poisoned his own wife. And while he was more than likely the guilty party, he used her death as an excuse to enact another round of terrible retribution on the boyars, accusing them of the same treachery they had committed against Anastasia. This time, with his *Oprichniki* willing to carry out any command that he wished, Ivan did not have any limits on his cruelty. He watched with satisfaction as hundreds of people were tortured and killed in a variety of cruel and horrific ways right in front of his eyes.

All of this had taken its toll on him. With every death, with every scream of agony that reached his ears, and with every act of unspeakable brutality that Ivan ordered and then watched with pleasure, his thirst for blood only grew. The circumstances that had so psychologically twisted him as a boy had only worsened, and Ivan was no longer content with maiming small animals or throwing pets from the roof of the castle. No, he needed to see thousands killed now; he needed to hear people scream. It was the only thing that seemed to settle him. The poor little boy that had been so thoroughly disturbed by his childhood had grown up into a monster.

And now, Novgorod was about to experience the full extent of Ivan's brutality and heartlessness. As he rode toward the city, Ivan knew that its clergy had already experienced thefts, executions, and torture for weeks. The surrounding towns had been pillaged and razed to the ground, and now, the population of Novgorod—already decimated by plague and now surrounded by the terrifying *Oprichniki*—could do little except await its horrible fate.

Ivan reined in his horse for a second, staring down at the city. Cold anger burned in his heart toward every living thing lying down there. He had accused its citizens of treason, fearing their defection to Polish Lithuania, his enemy in the Livonian War; it was conveniently located near the Russian border, and there was little to stop it from following in Kurbsky's footsteps and seeking greener pastures with a monarch whose head was screwed on straight. But Novgorod would never have that opportunity. Ivan would destroy it first.

Coldly, Ivan gave the order to charge. He set spurs to his horse, hefting his own weapon, and galloped straight for the city. It is difficult to conceive what was going through his mind at that moment. Was his mind empty and cold like a psychopath, his actions glittering with that icy calculation borne of a total lack of any form of empathy? Or was it tumultuous, chaotic, driven wild by one who had felt too much, who had endured too much pain and became a physical manifestation of that pain, inflicting it on hundreds and thousands of other people in a desperate bid to escape its oppressive weight? Either way, the next few days of Ivan's life were the bloodiest of his entire reign. Personally leading his *Oprichniki* through the streets of Novgorod, he sought to sow destruction and agony wherever he rode. It was a move similar to the rampages he used to go on as a child, leading his rowdy band of buddies to trample on pedestrians. Except now he was not just a kid with a bunch of naughty friends. He was a tsar at the helm of a legion of vicious warriors ready to do his bidding, and he was out to kill.

To list all the atrocities committed by Ivan in the following days would fill chapters and chapters. To do justice to his victims, most of whom remain nameless and faceless to history as they were simply ordinary people going about innocent and ordinary lives, would be impossible. Women and children were raped. Houses were torched, and in the smoke of their burning, their inhabitants were skinned alive or hung or hacked to pieces by the bloodthirsty *Oprichniki* and their heartless leader. Animals were butchered in the streets alongside their owners. Windows were shattered or torn down, people were thrown into the river and drowned, and men and women were blown up with gunpowder, bits of their burnt and disintegrated corpses left scattered around the streets and trampled by the hooves of the *Oprichniki*'s horses as they chased down other victims. They captured the archbishop, and on Ivan's command, they sewed him into the skin of a freshly hunted bear. Its blood and flesh stuck to him and was smeared all over him, rotting and filthy, as the *Oprichniki* let him go and told him to run, laughing and jeering. The archbishop ran, and Ivan let loose his hunting dogs. They chased him down, and his screams echoed around the mountains as the pack ripped him apart.

It was a period of utter horror and a hell on earth for the inhabitants of Novgorod. Ivan unleashed the full force of his cruelty, and the aftermath was devastating. Over a period of about five weeks, somewhere between 15,000 and 60,000 people were brutally murdered for no good reason. Novgorod, once the pride of Russia, the jewel in its crown would take centuries to recover. Today, it has risen from the ashes of the massacre, survived the World Wars, and remains as a World Heritage Site under the new name of Veliky Novgorod (Novgorod the Great).

But in 1570, there was almost nothing left of it. Once Ivan was done with it, the city had been practically destroyed, most of its inhabitants killed. The full power and limitless cruelty of the *Oprichniki* and their leader had been put on display for the whole of Russia to see, and the smoking ruins of Novgorod were proof.

We can only speculate at how much more destruction may have taken place had the *Oprichniki* been allowed to continue. Yet they would remain for only two more years before meeting a foe that they could not hope to beat—and falling out of favor with Ivan as a result of their failure.

Chapter 12 – The Failure of the Oprichniki

The Crimean Tatars were coming, and Ivan knew that there was almost nothing he could do.

Heading his *Oprichniki*, Ivan watched in horror as the massive force of Tatars headed straight for him. They were only a few miles away from Moscow, within a day's march of the capital, and Ivan was never supposed to have engaged with his enemy. He had led his handful of *Oprichniki* out more as a show of solidarity than with any goal of actually doing battle; the *Zemshchina* force sent out ahead of him was supposed to do all of the real fighting. Ivan preferred to kill things that did not fight back. But now, he was faced with a Tatar army 40,000 strong, led by the formidable Tatar Khan Devlet I Giray. The *Zemshchina* force that had been sent to guard the river Oka against the approaching horde had failed. Russian traitors, desperate to see anyone but Ivan ruling over their country, had smuggled the entire Crimean force across the river without any opposition, and now they were flooding across the landscape, heading directly for Ivan and his little army.

The spring countryside was pitch black, teeming with the vast numbers of Tatars. Their swift, shaggy ponies could gallop for miles, bearing archers whose accuracy and speed were a deadly combination; they could reload much faster than cannons and approach and retreat with remarkable speed and agility, making them lethal even when faced with more modern weapons. Looking back over the black-clad riders on their shining black horses, Ivan saw fear in their eyes. Suddenly the force that had so easily razed Novgorod almost to the ground no longer seemed so mighty. The *Oprichniki* had never tasted real war. Within the safe confines of the *Oprichnina*, they had met with no opposition, instead persecuting unarmed peasants and panicking commoners. They were neither trained for war nor seasoned by it, and Ivan knew, with sudden clarity, that to lead them against the Tatars would be nothing short of suicide.

While Kurbsky would be quick to chalk up Ivan's next action to nothing but cowardice, the tsar was out of options. He knew that the Tatars would mow down his little force as if it had never existed. Wheeling his horse around, he shouted to his army to retreat. They didn't need to be told twice. Setting heels to their horses, the *Oprichniki* fled as fast as their horses could carry them. They rode hard to the north, having to take a detour around Moscow since they knew it was the true target of the Tatar invasion. Ivan knew that most of his army was fighting in Livonia; the majority of the *strelski*—the standing army—that remained in Russia was now waiting around on the banks of the Oka, their enemy having long since gone. The garrison that was left in Moscow was a skeleton of a skeleton crew, decimated by plague and the demands of the Livonian War. Only 6,000 men strong, it didn't stand a chance against the Tatars. Moscow was going to fall, and Ivan knew it, but he did little to try to stop the inevitable disaster. He just spurred his horse on and rode as hard as he could for Aleksandrovskaya Sloboda.

The tsar sheltered there in his hunting lodge-turned-fortress as the Tatars continued, inexorably and relentlessly, toward Moscow. The hapless commander of the Moscow garrison had little option but to lead his army out, knowing that it was doomed before the fighting began. The Tatars barely slowed down. Crushing the Muscovite army effortlessly, they pushed onward, reaching the suburbs of the city almost unopposed. The hundreds of thousands of civilians inside Moscow were helpless. They could only watch as Devlet I Giray had the nearest houses soaked in oil and then touched a blazing torch to the slick surfaces. Flame after flame rushed into the air as the Tatars galloped down the streets to screams and panic, lighting up the houses. Bedrooms and kitchens, backyards and stables went up in flames; the water barrels on the roofs that Ivan had implemented decades ago did little to slow down the fiery chaos. When a sudden wind came out of nowhere, it seized the fire and flung it up toward the Kremlin. Roaring, the fire was whipped up into a frenzy, devouring whole blocks at a time as it rushed upon the teeth of the wind. Panicking citizens flung themselves into the river or hid in stone buildings, which collapsed under the heat of the fire and the force of the wind it had created. They perished in the thousands, and so did those who drowned in the river or were not lucky enough to escape the flames.

In six hours, most of Moscow was destroyed. The palace had burned to the ground, and acres of suburbs were reduced to nothing but ashes. Thousands of people—guesses range around 60,000—had died. The tragedy of the Great Fire of 1547 had been repeated, except this time, it was magnified and made much worse by the fact that this was no sad accident. This could have been prevented, but treachery and the failure of the *Oprichniki* had left the Tatars unopposed, and Moscow had to pay the price. The betrayal that Ivan had always feared had taken place, but his people had paid for it while he was safely tucked away in his fortress at Sloboda. As for the Tatars, they disappeared, carried by their fleet-footed little ponies back to the land from whence they came. Their losses could not have been significant.

The 1571 Fire of Moscow dwarfed the Great Fire of 1547, and like that early disaster, it finally spurred Ivan into action. Realizing that the *Oprichniki* had failed to protect him or Russia from outside invasions—or from the treachery that had made the Crimean raid so successful—Ivan decided that they were more trouble than they were worth. Over the next year, he would continue to mull over this decision, but in 1572, the *Oprichniki* was disbanded and the *Oprichnina* was abolished. In an ironic twist that the senior *Oprichnik* officers could never have seen coming, Ivan executed them for failing to protect him and his capital.

As for the Crimean Tatars, they came back the next summer, aiming to repeat their raid of 1571 and perhaps even to invade and claim Moscow instead of merely burning it. However, they were met with a strong Russian army led by Prince Mikhail Vorotynsky. Despite the fact that the prince only commanded half the number of men that the Crimean leader did, when they met on the banks of the Lopasnya, a week-long battle ensued that would take a heavy toll on both sides. Ivan himself was holed up in Novgorod at the time and gave orders to Vorotynsky, but he did not actively participate in the battle itself. It ended in a decisive victory for the Russians, and the Tatars were beaten back to such an extent that neither they nor their Turkish allies would attempt any more raids on Russia during Ivan's reign.

Vorotynsky was welcomed back as a hero of the war—perhaps with too much enthusiasm by a people desperate for a true hero. He was greatly celebrated for about a year before Ivan grew jealous of his popularity, accused him of infringing on the throne, and personally tortured him to death.

* * * *

Now in his forties, Ivan had become a widower for the second time in 1569 after the death of Maria. This time, he would take two years to replace her. Perhaps he was reluctant to return to matrimony after his unhappy union with Maria, or perhaps he was simply too busy causing chaos within his own country. Either way, in 1571, he finally settled on his third wife. This time, he was once again allured by youth and beauty and once again avoided marrying into any of the boyar families that he so detested.

Marfa Vasilevna Sobakina was the nineteen-year-old daughter of a merchant. After an extensive bride-show, Ivan had chosen twelve finalists; Marfa, he decided eventually, was the most beautiful of them all. He must have been aware that she would be his last wife as the Orthodox Church stipulated that only three marriages would be allowed, regardless of what happened to the previous spouses. His wedding day with Marfa was supposed to be his last.

Sadly, however, their union was doomed even before it began. Marfa's mother had never dreamed that her young daughter would someday become the Tsaritsa of Russia; traditionally, only princesses and those of the noblest blood were chosen to marry grand princes. It was only because of Ivan's abhorrence of the boyar families that a common girl like Marfa had been chosen, and her family suddenly found itself elevated to a nearly royal status. Marfa's mother's imagination ran wild. She imagined one of her grandchildren upon the throne of Russia one day, and so as Marfa prepared for the wedding ceremony, her mother started to give her doses of an elixir that she'd been told would make her daughter more fertile.

Tragically, the elixir was far from a fertility potion. Instead, it was something deadly—a poison whose identity has since been lost. The more of the potion that Marfa drank, the more the weight melted off her, her flesh shrinking on her bones until she could barely stand on her wedding day, a hollow-eyed skeleton of the bright girl that Ivan had chosen. Nonetheless, the ceremony went ahead, even though Marfa swayed where she stood at the altar. Ivan took her home to the impregnable fortress of Aleksandrovskaya Sloboda, certain that she would be safe with him inside those formidable walls and surrounded only by hand-picked attendants of whose loyalty Ivan was absolutely certain. Yet it was not enough. The damage had already been done, and Marfa was not safe from whatever lethal substance was eating her up from the inside out. Within days of their wedding, she died.

Ivan went wild. He immediately accused the boyars of poisoning Marfa, although they would have been utter fools to even attempt such a thing. Once again, the boyars faced a wave of executions and tortures as Ivan sent out his *Oprichniki* on their last rampage before they were disbanded. Even the family of Anastasia, his beloved first wife, was not safe. Her brother was impaled and killed for the crime of poisoning Marfa, even though it is extremely unlikely that he actually committed the crime.

By now, such cruelty was second nature to Ivan, automatic and effortless, especially with the *Oprichniki* at his disposal; yet even after they were disbanded in 1572—about a year after Marfa's death—Ivan continued to act with suspicion and hatred toward those closest to him. His people felt a surge of hope when he abolished the *Oprichnina* (even banning the use of the very word *Oprichnina*), thinking that perhaps their ruler had returned to some form of lucidity. Yet Ivan would soon prove that the end of the *Oprichnina* was not the end of his madness. It was just another step forward in his slow and unstoppable slide into total insanity.

* * * *

Soon after the end of the *Oprichnina* and having recently married his fourth wife, Anna Alexeievna Koltovskaya, Ivan seemed to be lost. Without his *Oprichniki* to sow chaos at his bidding and without the loyal followers that had made up the *Oprichnina* around him, Ivan didn't know what to do with himself. He had been able to occupy himself for a little while by persecuting random people whom he believed were to blame for the death of Marfa, but now, he felt directionless. In fact, he was tired of tsardom, tired of the constant worry over his life and the lives of those closest to him, and tired—it may be speculated—of life. For all the atrocities Ivan had committed, not a single one had managed to make him happy. He had done whatever he'd wanted, and nothing had made him feel better. He continued to be a profoundly disturbed and deeply depressed individual, and even at the relatively young age of forty-two, he had straggling gray hairs and deep wrinkles that made him look twice his own age.

Ivan was sick of ruling over Russia, regardless of how poorly he had been doing so for the past several years. So, he did what he had tried to do almost a decade ago: He abdicated. Only this time, instead of leaving the throne to the boyars, he decided to place a new tsar of his own choosing upon the throne that he didn't want. Despite the fact that his son and heir, Ivan Ivanovich, was already eighteen years old—a little older than Ivan himself had been when he had been crowned Tsar of All the Russias—Ivan elected not to place him on the throne. Instead, he chose a fairly obscure former Tatar general named Simeon Bekboelatovitch.

Little is known about Bekboelatovitch's "reign" other than the fact that it appears that it was not official. He was nothing but a puppet in Ivan's hands, a hapless—and probably terrified—individual who did little other than keep the seat of the throne warm for Ivan's inevitable return. For a year, Ivan lived at one of his country estates in luxury and relaxation, although what exactly was going through his mind at that point in time is impossible to even guess at. Frequently, he would ride to Moscow to pay homage to his new "tsar," bowing down before Bekboelatovitch and showing him submission and loyalty. Russia teetered on the brink of disaster, its government having never been more uncertain than now. As frightening as Ivan had been in recent years, it was a relief for most Russians when he suddenly grew tired of this charade and reclaimed the throne. Surprisingly, Bekboelatovitch was not harmed. He was given lands and a noble title, and he was allowed to carry on with his life while Ivan resumed the throne.

The tsar had now reached the last decade of his reign. He had both caused and endured an almost incomprehensible amount of suffering, but the worst of it all was still to come. Ivan's family was in danger, and this time, it was from the patriarch himself.

Chapter 13 – Two Killings

Illustration VIII: Ivan the Terrible and His Son Ivan on 16 November 1581*, an emotive depiction of the death of Tsarevich Ivan Ivanovich by Ilya Repin*

The 1570s were a tumultuous decade for Ivan. Starting with the Massacre of Novgorod, continuing with the Fire of Moscow and then the end of the *Oprichnina*, and followed by the death of Marfa, Ivan's circumstances were as unstable and wild as his mood swings. And as the decade wore on, things would only get worse.

In 1572, shortly after Marfa's untimely demise, Ivan went on to marry his fourth wife, Anna Koltovskaya. This union was not accepted by the Church and only barely accepted by the people when Ivan appeased them by saying that he had not had the time to consummate his marriage to Marfa due to her sickness and rapid death. Either way, it appears that Ivan was past caring what the Church or anyone else thought of him as long as nobody was poisoning his wives. Anna herself was, as usual for Ivan's wives, not of high birth; she must have been a young woman or even a girl when Ivan married her, for while her date of birth has been lost, she would outlive Ivan, dying in 1626. However, their marriage would not survive as long as Anna did. She proved to be infertile. After two years of marriage, in 1574, Ivan tired of her. Instead of poisoning her as he likely did with his second wife Maria, he simply sent her off to a convent to become a nun. She took the veil as Sister Daria and may later have been canonized as Saint Daria in the Eastern Orthodox Church.

Details on what happened next in Ivan's marital life are sketchy. He married again in 1575, even though this wedding was most certainly frowned upon by the Church; this wife, another Anna, did not last long before meeting the same end as Anna Koltovskaya. Anna the second, however, may have been murdered in the convent—most of the details about her life have since been lost to the creeping fog of time.

Ivan's sixth wife, Vasilisa Melentyeva, most likely did not exist. A figment of 19th-century imaginations, Vasilisa allegedly arrived in Moscow as a widow seeking shelter and became Ivan's wife. She fell in love with a prince, and when Ivan found out, the prince was impaled and Vasilisa sent to a convent. No historical evidence can be found that points toward Vasilisa's existence; her story was more than likely fabricated. She was supposedly Ivan's wife for a brief few months during 1579.

Maria Dolgorukaya is also likely to be nothing more than a legend. Fabled to be Ivan's seventh wife, she was also accused of infidelity, but her story does not end as peacefully as Vasilisa's. Instead of being sent to the convent, legend has it that Maria was drowned. Her existence has not been confirmed.

Finally, in 1581, Ivan married for the eighth time—and this time his spouse actually did exist. Maria Nagaya was spared the fate of her predecessors when she produced a son for Ivan in 1582, a little boy who was named Dmitri.

Dmitri was a small piece of good news. But the events of the previous year of 1581 in Ivan's family had been bad—very, very bad.

* * * *

Since retaking the throne after the brief and peculiar reign of the Tatar general, Ivan had been largely inactive in affairs of the state. He made a few attempts to reform something similar to the *Oprichnina* in a bid to protect himself, but none had been as notorious as the *Oprichnina* itself, and the *Oprichniki* would never come together again. Apart from this, Ivan all but withdrew himself from the duties that came with the throne. Yet there was one aspect of his reign that could not be ignored: the Livonian War.

Ever since Lithuania had become involved in the war, the Russian forces had been suffering continual defeats. For two decades now, the opposing armies had been struggling in a drawn-out series of skirmishes and battles that had cost thousands of lives. Refugees fleeing the war had poured into Russia and even into Moscow itself, bringing with them horrendous outbreaks of the plague. Russia could not support the vast number of mouths it now suddenly had to feed, and famine resulted. Yet Ivan refused to engage in peace talks with the Livonians. Instead, he allowed the fighting to drag on.

This was a terrible mistake. Once Livonia had been won back entirely, Ivan's enemies set their sights on a greater target: Russia itself. They knew that trying to negotiate peace meant nothing now—Ivan would stubbornly continue trying to wage this war until something gave. Invasion was the only option. In 1581, the Lithuanian army and its allies laid siege to Pskov, a Russian city not far from the border of Livonia. Despite the fact that it was defended by a large number of seasoned *strelski* soldiers, Pskov soon found itself struggling to survive the siege. Its commanders sent desperate messages to Moscow, begging for help to liberate the city.

If it was up to Ivan himself, the cries would have fallen on deaf ears. Instead, they reached his son, Ivan Ivanovich. Ivanovich had always been close with his father, and he had spent a lot of time with him— including participating in the Massacre of Novgorod when he was only a teenage boy—but when he heard about the trouble that Pskov was in, he decided that he would have to disagree with Ivan's decision to do nothing.

When Ivanovich first started to argue with him over the fate of Pskov, Ivan was heartbroken. His son had been his closest and most constant friend over the years; the one person that he had not lost. Anastasia had been poisoned decades ago, Kurbsky had betrayed him, and his wives had been a long string of failure after failure. But Ivanovich—he alone remained, and he alone was precious and treasured in Ivan's heart. He had stayed with his father despite his madness, and Ivan loved him more than anything else in the world.

This is not to say that Ivan had treated young Ivanovich well. He had married the boy off to a suitable young Swedish lady named Virginia Eriksdotter when Ivanovich was only a teenager, but when the couple failed to produce any children within a couple of years, Ivan promptly condemned his daughter-in-law to be imprisoned in a convent. Ivanovich's second wife, Praskovia Solova, was similarly incapable of producing a child. Ivan's solution to her infertility was as simple as it had always been for his own wives; off to the nunnery she went, and Ivan quickly found his son another girl to marry. Ivanovich was heartbroken at having his spouses so brutally stripped away from him, but he knew better than to argue with his father. As much as he missed his previous two wives, he meekly agreed to marry Yelena Sheremeteva. A few months Ivanovich's senior,

Yelena was luckier than his other wives had been. It was with great relief that the young couple discovered in October 1581 that Yelena was pregnant with Ivanovich's first child.

Now, at last, Ivanovich hoped he and his wife would be left alone to enjoy their marriage and children together. But it was not to be. Ivan's insanity was about to take a terrible swing for the worse, a swing that would not only change Ivanovich's life: It would take it.

* * * *

Yelena was terrified of her father-in-law.

She hardly dared to move as she sat in the same room as he did. Even though she was almost too scared to look at him, she found herself sneaking glances to make sure that he was still sitting quietly in his chair. He was going bald on the top of his head; what was left of his hair hung down around his shoulders, white with stress and ragged where he had torn some of it away in one of his wild moods. His beard was similarly ruined, and his face was deeply lined, a mask of suffering amid the finery of his clothing. His eyes were the worst though. They were sunken deep into the dark sockets of his skull so that they were little more than a black glitter somewhere among the shadows in his face, their expression unreadable. His entire posture seemed to emanate hatred and despair. It was like sitting with a black hole of emotional energy that sucked at Yelena's vibrant youth.

She had not been given a choice in marrying Ivanovich. Arranged marriage was the only fate awaiting most young noblewomen of the period, and as the daughter of a boyar, Yelena would have been expecting something along these lines to happen to her eventually. Yet she dreaded the very idea of becoming part of Tsar Ivan's household. He had murdered thousands of boyars; it's more than likely that members of Yelena's own family had succumbed to his wrath. And now she was sitting in the same room as he was, trying not to attract his attention.

But it was already too late. Suddenly, his mood snapping like a cracked whip, Ivan flew to his feet. Yelena cowered in place, her hands subconsciously moving over her pregnant belly, instinctively protecting her unborn baby as Ivan's mouth opened and launched an angry tirade that left Yelena feeling stunned. He had taken sudden and terrible objection to the clothes that Yelena was wearing; despite the wintry November weather outside, it was warm inside the palace, and Yelena had dressed lightly in accordance with the temperature. Yet something about her clothes had triggered Ivan's paranoia. He ranted at her, telling her that she was dressed promiscuously, that she was planning to cheat on his oldest son. Perhaps some of Ivan's fears that Ivanovich himself was infertile—not the wives that he had sent to the convents—came to the surface now as he accused Yelena of unspeakable things to her young ears. Panicking, Yelena protested that she had done no wrong, but Ivan could not be pacified. He flew at her, seizing her in a surprisingly strong grip considering his sickly appearance, and threw her to the floor. Yelena fell with an impact that almost stunned her. Showing no mercy, Ivan started to kick her, pummeling her body ruthlessly. All that Yelena could do was to curl up over her belly in a desperate attempt to protect her baby and scream as loudly as she could.

Ivanovich heard the screams. Rushing from elsewhere in the palace, he burst into the room to behold an utterly horrifying sight. His beautiful young wife was curled up on the floor, her hands thrown up to protect her face. Towering over her, his face twisted in a senseless anger that was baser and more brutal than that of the most savage animal, stood Ivan. He was kicking her, beating her, striking her with the butt of his scepter. And as Ivanovich stared in horror, he saw blood soaking into Yelena's skirt, running down over her thighs and seeping into the carpet.

Ivanovich snapped. He had not been given to the same fits of anger as his father, but his temper was lost now, and he flew into the room, shouting at the top of his lungs. "You sent my first wife to a convent for no reason!" Grabbing Ivan, he yanked him back, pulling him off

Yelena. Placing himself between his wife and his father, Ivanovich went on. "You did the same with my second. And now you strike the third!" He gestured furiously at Yelena where she began to sit up. Her bleeding was so profuse from between her legs that her dress was already soaked through with blood. Ivanovich's voice was an agonized whisper. "Causing the death of the son she holds in her womb."

Yelena raised a blood- and tear-stained face to her husband. They both knew what had just happened: Yelena had suffered a miscarriage of her and Ivanovich's child.

It is uncertain exactly when the following events took place. It may have been days later after Ivanovich had helped Yelena to her chambers and a physician had the chance to confirm that she had, indeed, lost her baby. It may have been in that very moment while Yelena lay bleeding on the carpet and Ivanovich stood over her in trembling rage. Either way, Ivan and Ivanovich began to argue. The topic of their shouting rants turned from Yelena and Ivanovich's other wives to Pskov and Ivanovich's vociferous opinion that Ivan should have liberated it long ago. Furious and heated with emotion, Ivan accused his son of plotting a rebellion. Ivanovich passionately declared his loyalty but held firm: Pskov needed help, and leaving it to the Livonians was heartless and pointless.

Finally, Ivan lost his temper entirely. Screaming incoherently in fury, he swung his iron scepter, a deadly instrument that had killed many an unlucky subject. This time, its target was his son. The point of the scepter thudded home to Ivanovich's temple. There was a terrible crack, a sound of shattering and crunching bone. A look of surprise and agony crossed the young man's face for a moment, and then, his knees buckled, and he crumpled to the floor.

The horror of what he had just done struck Ivan immediately, snapping him out of his psychotic rage. With a howl of remorse, he flung himself to the ground, frantically scooping his boy into his arms. Ivanovich was limp, blood pouring down the side of his face from a wound in his temple. His head looked dented, crushed where the scepter had struck home. His movements shaking with fear, Ivan tried to stop the bleeding, pressing his bony hand to the wound. He cuddled Ivanovich against him, begging him to live. "May I be damned!" he moaned. "I've killed my son. I've killed my son!"

His words were not untrue. Ivanovich's skull was shattered. He would linger for a few more days in a coma, lying as still as death in his chamber. Finally, on November 19th, 1581, Tsarevich Ivan Ivanovich of Russia died.

Ivan's grief over the death of Ivanovich equaled his feelings after Anastasia died. He screamed and howled, overcome with remorse for what he had done in his fit of senseless rage. When he saw Ivanovich's coffin for the first time, he lost all reason. Seizing its edge, he beat his head against it until his skin broke and blood poured down his face. Then he continued to scream, staggering around the palace like a wounded animal, unable to comprehend or feel anything other than his terrible grief. His own cruelty and inability to control his emotions had come back to bite him in the most agonizing way possible.

Chapter 14 – The Legacy of Ivan "The Terrible"

Illustration IX: A sculpture of Ivan by Mark Antokolski

Stripped naked and used for target practice by the *Oprichniki*. Sewn in a bearskin and torn apart by hungry dogs. Doused in alternating boiling and freezing water until the skin ruptured. Hanging. Drowning. Boiling in a cauldron. Ribs plucked out by red-hot tongs.

Decapitation. Trampled by wild ponies. Struck by a scepter. These are just some of the gruesome ways that Ivan's victims had been murdered, from the hapless peasants of Novgorod to the hated boyars to his own child. But Ivan himself, ironically, would be spared any kind of a gruesome death. His own demise would be strangely peaceful—although possibly self-inflicted in a strangely roundabout way.

Ivan was fifty-four years old, and ever since the death of his son, he had been more or less simply waiting to die. The Livonian War had been lost; Maria Nagaya had given birth to Ivan's last child, Dmitri, in 1582; and now, in the year 1584, Ivan had become a sickly and shambling shell of the tyrant that he once was. He was still capable of ordering great violence, but he could now no longer dispense any of it himself. Disease had seeped into his very bones; his joints were failing him even though he was not an old man yet, and he had to be carried on a litter everywhere that he wished to go. Even his skin was bursting open to reveal sores that oozed a foul-smelling pus.

Russia itself was on the verge of economic collapse. The Livonian War had been incredibly expensive. It had sucked the economy dry, a process expedited by the droughts, famines, and plagues that the nation had endured and made worse by the fact that—with Ivan sick and the boyars decimated by his persecution—there was little in the way of a government in Russia. The only flicker of good news during that time was the fact that one brave soldier named Yermak Timofeevich, a former brigand, had taken up his sword and sought a new frontier on the border of Russia and Siberia. Working for the Stroganov family, who had been colonizing the barren area, Yermak had succeeded in driving out the Mongols who had then occupied Siberia. He conquered the area for Russia and became a hero in the eyes of the people.

Ivan honored Yermak with a title and the Stroganovs with gifts of land, but the good news did little to distract him from the reality that he knew was coming ever closer. His death was not far off, and he knew it. Somehow, he managed to scrape together enough rational thinking to write his will, which was a grim document in and of itself. With Ivan dead, the throne of Russia would fall to the mentally handicapped Feodor, but there was no other choice; Dmitri was only two years old, and Ivan couldn't bear for the little boy to suffer the same fate that he had as the Grand Prince of Moscow without a father, tortured in the Kremlin by the boyars. He left the principality of Uglich to Dmitri instead, the same territory that had been ruled over by Ivan's deaf-mute brother Yuri before his death several years ago. There were no two ways about it—Feodor would have to become the tsar, whether he was suitable for the position or not.

That was where Ivan's rationality ended. The fears that had always followed him were closing in on him now, tightening around him like a hungry circle of starving dogs, ready to rip him to shreds the way that his own pack of hounds had torn Andrei Shuisky limb from limb and given Ivan his first taste for murder. Now even murder could not take his mind off the fact that he knew he was dying, and he was scared—scared and alone. For the first time, Ivan turned his back on the church. Seeking help from a darker quarter, he sent for sixty Lapp magicians to work their witchcraft on him in a bid to save him.

Of course, the magicians could do nothing to help the tsar feel better. According to legend, however, they could predict his death: March 18th, 1584. They gave this information to Bogdan Belsky, then Ivan's friend and favorite. Belsky, however, was hoping that he would inherit the throne, so he kept the information quiet. Instead, he attempted to take the tsar's mind off his impending death by keeping him occupied with what recreational activities he could engage in considering his infirm state.

As a boy, Ivan had hunted down peasants in the street and ridden wildly through the countryside. Raping and pillaging had been his idea of fun. Now, however, he could no longer walk, let alone ride. He was left with little to do except play chess.

It was March 18th, 1584, the date that the Lapp magicians had said would be Ivan's last day on this earth. Belsky was uneasy, but he tried his best to hide it. Perhaps the magicians had been wrong after all. As Belsky waited for the tsar in his bedchamber, he could hear Ivan singing in the bath; he had just been given his medicine, and he seemed to be feeling better that day.

When Ivan was helped into his room, Belsky noticed that his cheeks had some color to them. He seemed cheerful enough, dressed comfortably in a loose gown, and when he sat down on his bed, he called for a game of chess instead of going straight to bed as he usually did. The chessboard was brought out, and Ivan asked Belsky to play a game with him.

What happened next is still not entirely clear. Some accounts say that Ivan had only managed to place the chess pieces on the board when the attack seized him; others report that he and Belsky played a full game and that Belsky had won, prompting Ivan to rise from his bed in a fit of thoughtless rage. Either way, as Ivan handled the pieces, Belsky noticed that he seemed to be fumbling with them a little, as if he didn't have control over his own hands. Perhaps his speech slurred somewhat, too; his face may have begun to droop, and then, with a suddenness that shocked Belsky and the other attendants in the room, Ivan collapsed. He flopped onto the bed, his heavy body causing the pillows to bounce as it crashed down onto the mattress, a limp weight. Belsky shot to his feet. Ivan had been fainting more and more often over the years, a symptom of his numerous diseases, but Belsky could see that this time was different. The tsar's face was ashen; his breaths came in rasping, rattling gasps, and his limbs twitched wildly as vomit started to trickle from the corner of his mouth.

Panic filled the room. Belsky swung around, bellowing for Ivan's physicians and apothecaries to be brought. People scurried in and out among Belsky's shouted orders as Ivan gasped and choked on the bed, strangled noises dribbling from his slack mouth. The smells of bodily fluids filled the air, followed by the herbal scents of the remedies that the physicians brought in as they rushed to tend to the tsar. Sadly, with no other method to administer the medicine except orally, all the physicians likely could have done was help Ivan choke to death faster. After a few minutes of horror, Ivan gave a last, agonized gasp and then stopped. Silence fell in the room, and when the attending physician looked up, he was pale. Everyone knew at once that Ivan was dead. The first Tsar of All the Russias, the terror of the boyars, the scourge of Novgorod, was gone from this world forever.

* * * *

Ivan's cause of death was most likely a stroke brought on, perhaps, by the stress of losing his chess game. Speculations that he was poisoned by his enemies appear to have been unfounded; although an excavation and investigation of his body in the 1960s revealed a fairly high concentration of mercury in his tissues, this was a common remedy at the time used to treat arthritic joints. It was also used for syphilis, which may have contributed to his death as well.

Ivan had wished to become a monk before his death in the same way as Vasili, his father, had, but it was so sudden that he never had the chance. Instead, a well-meaning clergyman dressed his dead body in a monk's habit and renamed him Iona, giving Ivan his wish a few minutes too late.

Thousands of people all across Russia would have been elated to hear that Ivan was gone. Even his wife Maria could hardly have been blamed for feeling relief over his death, and it was certainly a great relief to the boyars who could finally rest from the persecution they had been enduring for decades. When the news reached the convent where Daria, formerly Ivan's wife Anna, had been sent, she must have felt a sense of satisfaction that the man who had so mistreated her was gone at last. But one person was utterly devastated by his death, and that was his son Feodor. He came into the chamber to find his father lying there then fell onto the bed beside him. Hugging the cold body of his father to his own infirm, warm, living flesh, he cried inconsolably. Feodor may have been a grown man, but he had the mental faculties of a child; he must have known about his father's atrocities, but all he cared about in that moment was the fact that his dad was gone.

If Feodor had known what was to come, he would have wept all the more. Despite a regent of four advisers that Ivan had appointed before his death, Feodor's reign was to be an ignominious one; helpless to do anything to stop the decline of his father's empire, Feodor could do little but watch as Russia descended into chaos.

As for Ivan himself, his body was laid in an open coffin to be viewed by the masses. Even though he had been a terrible tyrant, the sight was enough to move many of his people to tears. Ivan had been tsar for thirty-seven years—most of Russia's people had never known another emperor, and they feared the time that was yet to come.

Ivan's body was laid to rest at last in the Cathedral of the Archangel in Moscow. His grave was side by side with that of his own son, Tsarevich Ivan. And there they lie still, the father who had killed his son and the young man whose death would result in the decline of Russia, the last testament to the rage and heartbreak that filled the life of Ivan Vasilyevich, Tsar of All the Russias.

Conclusion

Even after his death, Ivan would continue to cause controversy. His very name has been cause for confusion; although he was most certainly what we would call a terrible monarch by modern standards, his Russian name is Ivan Grozny. "Grozny" translates best into the original use of the English word "terrible": to inspire terror. It was only after Ivan became widely known as "the Terrible" that the word "terrible" took on its modern-day connotations of badness or evil. "Grozny" would today translate into "fearsome" or "awe-inspiring."

Yet there is no arguing that Ivan's reign was a time of terror, a *terrible* time indeed for most Russians, specifically the boyar families. The evil that he committed is almost incomprehensible. Exactly how many people he was directly responsible for murdering is difficult to assess, but it is certainly in the thousands. Perhaps in the tens of thousands. Perhaps more.

Equally incomprehensible, however, is the suffering that Ivan had to endure as a child. His early years were characterized by luxury and security; as a small child, he would have known that he would be the Grand Prince of Moscow one day and that he would have everything he could possibly want. He would be the most powerful person in the length and breadth of Russia. But the brutal deaths of both his parents plunged his life into perfect darkness. Trying desperately to survive, to protect his deaf-mute brother, and to escape the warring boyars that were so determined to mistreat him, Ivan was just a little kid all alone. The scars that that time left on his psyche would haunt him forever, and when Anastasia died as horribly as she did, it left a raw wound that never quite healed.

And neither did the wounds that Ivan inflicted on Russia. He had caused its economy to fall apart during his own reign, and the fact that he had killed his heir would lead to even greater disaster a few years later. Feodor's reign marked the end of the Rurikid dynasty. He died childless in 1598, and his younger half-brother Dmitri had already died suspiciously a few years earlier. There was no heir to the Russian throne. This precipitated an era of such chaos and economic collapse that even Ivan's reign could not compare to. It would become known as the Time of Troubles, and it only came to an end when Mikhail Romanov—a descendant of Anastasia's family—was made tsar in 1613. This was the start of the Romanov dynasty which lasted for a little over three hundred years.

Ivan the Terrible was a murderer. He was a rapist, a killer, a dictator, a tyrant, an appalling monarch, and, some would say, a monster. Yet his monstrosity stemmed from agony, his violence from fear. Ivan was a frightening presence and a blight on the face of Russian history, but he was also, above all, a human being. His story is not some horror novel but a cautionary tale about the potential power of child abuse. As a kid, Ivan was just a little boy who was being treated badly. But as an adult, he became a looming threat to all of Russia.

Here's another book by Captivating History that we think you'd be interested in

And another one…

Sources

http://missinglink.ucsf.edu/lm/russia_guide/historyofrussia.htm#anci ent

https://www.britannica.com/topic/Rurik-dynasty

https://www.ancient.eu/Kievan_Rus/

https://www.britannica.com/topic/Kievan-Rus

https://www.britannica.com/place/Smolensk-Russia

http://www.newworldencyclopedia.org/entry/Kievan_Rus'

https://www.encyclopedia.com/history/modern-europe/russian-soviet-and-cis-history/kievan-rus

https://www.britannica.com/biography/Ivan-III

https://russiapedia.rt.com/prominent-russians/the-ryurikovich-dynasty/ivan-iii-the-great/

http://www.newworldencyclopedia.org/entry/Teutonic_Knights#Coa ts_of_arms

http://www.newworldencyclopedia.org/entry/Alexander_Nevsky

https://www.britannica.com/biography/Saint-Alexander-Nevsky

https://warfarehistorynetwork.com/daily/military-history/lake-peipus-battle-on-the-ice/

https://www.nationalgeographic.org/thisday/apr5/battle-ice/

Illustration I:
https://commons.wikimedia.org/wiki/File:Chorikov.jpg#/media/File:Chorikov.jpg

https://www.britannica.com/biography/Vasily-III

https://www.revolvy.com/page/Vasili-III-of-Russia

Illustration II:
https://upload.wikimedia.org/wikipedia/commons/7/71/Kolomen00.jpg

https://beautifulrus.com/elena-glinskaya-consort-of-moscow-regent/

https://www.revolvy.com/page/Elena-Glinskaya

https://www.historyofroyalwomen.com/elena-glinskaya/elena-glinskaya-poisoned-regent/

https://books.google.co.za/books?id=jfFaDwAAQBAJ&pg=PR128&lpg=PR128&dq=andrei+mikhailovich+shuisky&source=bl&ots=CJ-dZxSkcN&sig=ACfU3U3F-pVEmYqFxMaOldgF_ryVAor7fA&hl=en&sa=X&ved=2ahUKEwjzvY_SnYHhAhVROBoKHRZHAzwQ6AEwCHoECAAQAQ#v=onepage&q=andrei%20mikhailovich%20shuisky&f=false

Ivan the Terrible, by Ian Grey:
https://books.google.co.za/books?id=NpkrDQAAQBAJ&pg=PT44&lpg=PT44&dq=andrei+mikhailovich+shuisky+murder&source=bl&ots=KY5q_qf862&sig=ACfU3U1i9wanqLGXrz4XbmchcjDOWwd6Mg&hl=en&sa=X&ved=2ahUKEwi8y8ekn4HhAhUNbBoKHbT3CtoQ6AEwBnoECAEQAQ#v=onepage&q=andrei%20mikhailovich%20shuisky%20murder&f=false

rushist.com/index.php/platonov-en/1852-childhood-and-youth-of-ivan-the-terrible

Illustration IV: Wikipedia/Shakko
https://commons.wikimedia.org/wiki/File:Monomakh's_Cap_of_second_order_-_by_shakko_01.JPG

https://www.britannica.com/topic/Monomakhs-Cap

https://www.thevintagenews.com/2018/08/08/tsar-ivan-the-terrible-wifes/

https://www.encyclopedia.com/history/encyclopedias-almanacs-transcripts-and-maps/romanova-anastasia

https://owlcation.com/humanities/The-8-Wives-of-Ivan-The-Terrible

http://www.historyandwomen.com/2014/05/the-loss-of-anastasia-romanovna-ivans.html

https://www.biography.com/people/ivan-the-terrible-9350679

https://www.britannica.com/topic/zemsky-sobor

https://russianlife.com/stories/online/the-great-moscow-fire/

https://www.revolvy.com/page/Fire-of-Moscow-%281547%29

http://www.unm.edu/~ybosin/documents/mos_fire.pdf

Illustration V: By Erik Charlton.
https://commons.wikimedia.org/wiki/File:St._Basil's_Cathedral.jpg

http://mentalfloss.com/article/76266/12-facts-about-saint-basils-cathedral

https://www.historytoday.com/archive/kazan-falls-ivan-terrible

http://www.rusliterature.org/the-account-of-the-illness-of-ivan-the-terrible/#.XJNBOrPv7ak

https://www.thevintagenews.com/2017/06/23/poisonings-drowning-a-nunnery-or-exile-life-as-one-of-ivan-the-terribles-eight-wives/

https://www.telegraph.co.uk/news/worldnews/europe/russia/1326387/Mercury-poisoned-Ivan-the-Terribles-mother-and-wife.html

https://www.medicalnewstoday.com/articles/320563.php

Illustration VI: By Peter d'Aprix -
http://www.galleryhistoricalfigures.com, CC BY-SA 3.0,
https://commons.wikimedia.org/w/index.php?curid=9808691

http://russiasperiphery.blogs.wm.edu/transcaucasia/general/the-marriage-of-ivan-iv-and-maria-temryukovna/

https://www.britannica.com/biography/Sigismund-II-Augustus

https://www.encyclopedia.com/history/encyclopedias-almanacs-transcripts-and-maps/kurbsky-andrei-mikhailovich

http://smarthistories.com/andrey-kurbsky/

https://erenow.net/biographies/ivantheterriblepaynerobert/13.php

https://www.itinari.com/aleksandrovskaya-sloboda-the-residence-of-tsar-ivan-iv-the-terrible-2dk9

https://www.britannica.com/place/Veliky-Novgorod

Reign of Terror: Ivan IV, by Ruslan G. Skrynnikov:
https://books.google.co.za/books?id=UP7dCgAAQBAJ&pg=PA367&lpg=PA367&dq=sack+of+novgorod&source=bl&ots=hetVOPfd7V&sig=ACfU3U093QRvRiO9iUlVgKUD6441D-xEBw&hl=en&sa=X&ved=2ahUKEwiA_NvO4KHhAhWUrHEKHWxqDUMQ6AEwFXoECAgQAQ#v=onepage&q=sack%20of%20novgorod&f=false

https://historycollection.co/day-history-ivan-terrible-orders-massacre-novgorod-1570/

http://web-static.nypl.org/exhibitions/russia/Translation/punishment.html

https://therussianreader.com/tag/massacre-of-novgorod-1570/

https://www.rbth.com/arts/history/2017/08/04/dog-headed-people-what-was-ivan-the-terribles-oprichnina-force_816772

https://www.britannica.com/topic/oprichnina

https://www.warhistoryonline.com/history/molodinskaya-battle.html

Ivan the Terrible, by Maureen Perrie and Andrei Pavlov:
https://books.google.co.za/books?id=4YkABAAAQBAJ&pg=PT141&lpg=PT141&dq=1571+crimean+raid+on+moscow+oprichniki&so

urce=bl&ots=6w0rua8uQF&sig=ACfU3U32NtH4iyosneLfQT_krK
X964x2Eg&hl=en&sa=X&ved=2ahUKEwjwydeM-
aHhAhVUuHEKHdZaB2MQ6AEwGXoECAgQAQ#v=onepage&q
=1571%20crimean%20raid%20on%20moscow%20oprichniki&f=fal
se

https://www.revolvy.com/page/Fire-of-Moscow-%281571%29

Illustration VII: By Г. Седов. G. Sedov (1836-1884) -
http://picasaweb.google.com/beZprizornik/186/photo#51391440554
89612146, Public Domain,
https://commons.wikimedia.org/w/index.php?curid=3592433

http://www.rusartnet.com/biographies/russian-rulers/rurikid/family-
of-ivan-iv/wives/anna-koltovskaya

https://en.wikipedia.org/wiki/Tsarevich_Ivan_Ivanovich_of_Russia

http://enacademic.com/dic.nsf/enwiki/586081

https://people.howstuffworks.com/10-historically-pivotal-
murders1.htm

Illustration VIII: By Ilya Repin - Own work, Public Domain,
https://commons.wikimedia.org/w/index.php?curid=48908

http://www.historyofwar.org/articles/siege_pskov1582.html

https://www.methacton.org/cms/lib/PA01000176/Centricity/Domain
/121/ivan_the_terrible_reading_and_questions.pdf

https://www.ranker.com/list/crazy-things-done-by-ivan-the-
terrible/machk?page=2

*Royalty's Strangest Characters: Extraordinary But True Stories
From Two Thousand Years of Mad Monarchs and Raving Rulers*, by
Geoff Tibballs: https://books.google.co.za/books?id=nC-
_CAAAQBAJ&pg=PT90&lpg=PT90&dq=Simeon+Bekboelatovitch
&source=bl&ots=sWoW3PR_cD&sig=ACfU3U3fJ-
a4708E5PBuK0MKab5KAk84-
Q&hl=en&sa=X&ved=2ahUKEwiEnfyfyaThAhUeUhUIHa7yClkQ

6AEwAHoECAgQAQ#v=onepage&q=Simeon%20Bekboelatovitch
&f=false

https://www.revolvy.com/page/Marfa-Sobakina

https://owlcation.com/humanities/The-8-Wives-of-Ivan-The-Terrible

https://www.thevintagenews.com/2018/08/08/tsar-ivan-the-terrible-
wifes/

https://www.thoughtco.com/the-oprichnina-of-ivan-the-terrible-
3860937

Illustration IX: By No machine-readable author provided. Alex
Bakharev assumed (based on copyright claims). - No machine-
readable source provided. Own work assumed (based on copyright
claims).,   Public   Domain,
https://commons.wikimedia.org/w/index.php?curid=734692

https://russianlife.com/stories/online/ivan-the-terrible-tsar-of-all-
russias/

http://madmonarchs.guusbeltman.nl/madmonarchs/ivan4/ivan4_bio.
htm

https://www.thefamouspeople.com/profiles/ivan-the-terrible-
8647.php

https://www.revolvy.com/page/Ivan-the-Terrible

https://www.britannica.com/biography/Ivan-the-Terrible

https://russiapedia.rt.com/prominent-russians/the-ryurikovich-
dynasty/ivan-iv-the-terrible/

https://www.lingualift.com/blog/ivan-the-terrible/

https://allthatsinteresting.com/ivan-the-terrible

Printed in Great Britain
by Amazon